CLIMBING MASLOW'S PYRAMID

PAUL W. KING

CLIMBING MASLOW'S PYRAMID

Choosing your own path through life

First published 2009 (978-1848761-124)
Reprinted December 2011

The moral right of the author has been asserted.

Matador
5 Weir Road
Kibworth Beauchamp
Leicester LE8 0LQ, UK
Tel: 0116 279 2299
Email: books@troubador.co.uk
Web: www.troubador.co.uk/matador

ISBN 978 1848764 422

British Library Cataloguing in Publication Data.
A catalogue record for this book is available from the British Library.

Typeset in 11pt Stempel Garamond by Troubador Publishing Ltd, Leicester, UK
Printed in the UK by MPG Biddles, Kings Lynn

Matador is an imprint of Troubador Publishing Ltd

For Rocco
If you ever find anything of interest in this book or gain any insight from it, it will have been worth writing.

CONTENTS

ACKNOWLEDGMENTS   xi

INTRODUCTION   1
Abraham Maslow and his Pyramid   3

BUILDING THE FOUNDATIONS   9
Choosing your own path up Maslow's pyramid   11

    Where Do You Wish to Get to?   14
    Our Mental Health   17
    Self-Worth/Self-Esteem   19
    Do I Like the Person I am?   26
    Developing Self-Respect   28
    Self-Confidence   33

LEVELS 1 & 2 – BASIC LIFE NEEDS   43

    Biological/physiological and safety needs   45
    Physical Health   46
    Avoidable Illnesses   50
    Drugs – Use and Abuse   59
    The Food we Eat   64
    Fitness and Exercise   69
    Financial Freedom   72
    Money   81
    Do You Hate Paying Tax?   85

LEVEL 3 – BELONGING AND LOVE   89
Relating to Other People & the World Around Us

Relativity	91
Relationships	99
Touch	105
Sex	108
Fidelity	124
Partner Relationships	127
Finding that Relationship	134

LEVEL 4 – ESTEEM NEEDS   141
Achievement, status, responsibility, reputation

Need for Recognition	143
Releasing and Developing our True Personality	144
Fear, Frustration and Anger	149
Being Assertive	154
The Desire to be Attractive	158
Physical Attractiveness	164
Being Positive, Peaceful and Accepting	169
Personality, Attractiveness and Humour	174

LEVEL 5 – COGNITIVE NEEDS   183
Knowledge, meaning, self-awareness,
religious & spiritual choice

Ritual and Tradition	185
Faith	187
Religious Choice	189
Spirituality	197
Prayer and Meditation	200
Atheism	205
Preparation for Death	208

LEVEL 6 – AESTHETIC NEEDS 225
Beauty, balance, form

    Creativity and self-expression 227

LEVEL 7 – SELF-ACTUALISATION 233
Personal growth and fulfilment

    Some Foreign Words to Think About 235
    Forgiveness and Catharsis 238
    Integrity in Everyday Life 242
    Gratitude and Attitude 243
    Problem Solving – Decision Making 248
    Judgment and Common Sense 252
    Character Judgment 254
    Listening is as Important as Speaking 258
    Lifelong Learning 262
    Self-Actualization 266

LEVEL 8 – TRANSCENDENCE 269
Helping others to self-actualize

    Trancendence 271
    Final Thoughts 272

ABOUT THE AUTHOR 275

ACKNOWLEDGMENTS

I wish to acknowledge the enormous support and encouragement received from Jeni Sayer in the writing of this book. We discussed many of the issues and concepts covered and Jeni has been a constant source of inspiration.

My gratitude goes to Kate McNeilly for her wisdom and editing skills which have contributed so much to this book.

Finally, my thanks and gratitude go to the many people whose ongoing support and encouragement has been so invaluable.

INTRODUCTION

ABRAHAM MASLOW AND HIS PYRAMID

MASLOW'S HIERARCHY OF NEEDS

Dr Abraham Maslow was a prominent American psychologist who in the 1940's identified a simple and easily understandable set of needs that motivate all human beings.

Each of us is motivated by these needs, the most basic of which are inborn, having evolved over tens of thousands of years. Maslow's Hierarchy of Needs states that we must satisfy our most basic needs before moving on to the higher ones.

Only when the lower order needs of physical and emotional well-being are satisfied are we concerned with the higher order needs of influence and personal development.

Abraham Maslow depicted these levels of ascending human pursuit in the form of pyramid which became known as "Maslow's Hierarchy of Human Needs". A simplified form of this pyramid is shown on the next page.

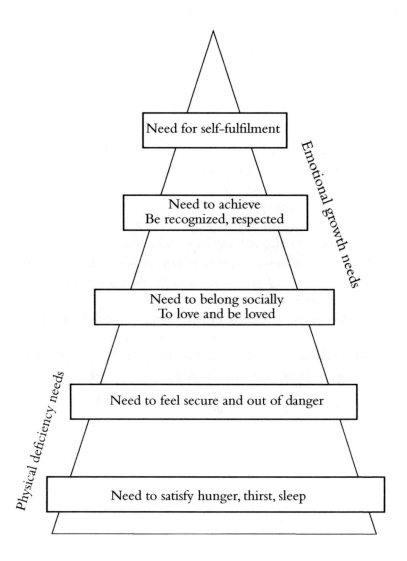

Maslow's Hierachy of Human Needs

Maslow's Hierarchy of Needs model as developed in the 1940-50's America remains valid today for understanding human motivation and personal development. At that time, the Hierarchy of Needs consisted of five levels. The original version is still considered by many to be the definitive hierarchy of needs.

In the 1970's the Hierarchy of Needs model was expanded to include cognitive and aesthetic needs, as follows:

1   Biological and physiological needs – air, food, drink, shelter, warmth, sex and sleep.
2   Safety needs - protection from elements, security, order, law, limits, stability, etc.
3   Belonging and Love needs – work group, family affection, relationships, etc.
4   Esteem needs – self-esteem, achievement, mastery, independence, dominance, prestige, managerial responsibility, etc.
5   Cognitive needs – community, meaning, etc.
6   Aesthetic needs – appreciation and search for beauty, balance, form, etc.
7   Self-actualization needs – realizing personal potential, self-fulfillment, seeking personal growth and peak experiences.

In the 1990's the Hierarchy of Needs was adapted further to include:

8   Transcendence needs – helping others to achieve self-actualization.

On the next page is an extended pyramid showing the additional levels.

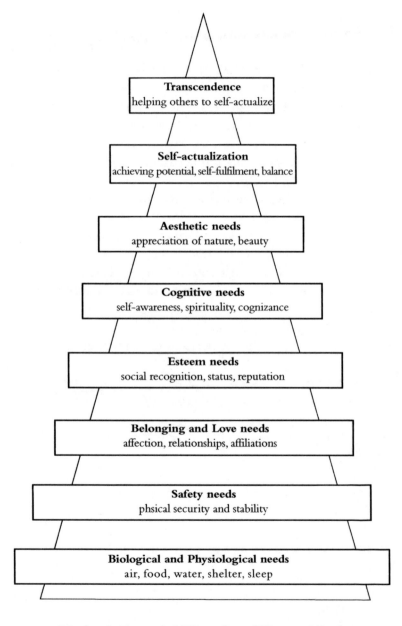

Maslow's Extended Hierachy of Human Needs

When our basic physiological needs have been met, we progress to a new set of needs which are less pressing for immediate survival but are nonetheless very important to us all.

We need to feel safe and secure, able to live with the belief that we are unlikely to come to physical harm. Put in another context, we could say that we need to feel financially secure which in turn may mean that we need to feel secure in our employment.

We have social needs and a natural inclination to be part of a group, to be accepted, to love and be loved, and to be sexual.

As human beings, we have an innate desire for recognition, we need to be respected, to be seen and heard and to have a position or status within our society.

When our basic needs have been met, we seek to understand, to be creative, to express ourselves, to be spiritual, to find a sense of achievement and self- fulfillment.

Moving away from the academic and theoretical, the following pages will look at issues which affect all of us - our self image, our confidence, our ability to develop relationships, our sexuality, our spirituality, and our health, both mental and physical.

This book is partly a retrospective account of my own journey. It shows the choices which I saw as being available to me and which are open to all of us, remembering that life is not static and that our views and opinions can, and do, change.

The intention of this book is to bring into focus, and perhaps give some insight into, those issues which are universal to us all - to look at some of the choices we can make in life which will affect our own happiness and in turn the happiness of all those people with whom we come into contact.

Let's look at some choices we have.

BUILDING THE FOUNDATIONS

CHOOSING OUR OWN PATH UP MASLOW'S PYRAMID

It has been said that medical science is giving us longer lives but no reason to live longer. In most developed countries, each generation is materially more affluent that the last. But the increase in wealth does not produce a corresponding increase in happiness. What is interesting is that the key questions which human beings have been asking themselves for generations are still as valid today as they always have been.

The key question is: What is the purpose of life? Or, more specifically, what is the purpose of my life?

The answer will lie in one of two directions. For those with religious beliefs, there is clear guidance. But for those without faith or those who are uncertain about their spiritual beliefs, the question itself becomes: "Given that I am alive, what do I want from life?" Often the vague response comes that "I want to be happy." But happiness itself is multi-faceted and must then be defined in order to be achievable.

Most of us drift through life on the tides of circumstance. The conditions of our childhood set the framework of our belief and value systems. Yet from young adulthood we are in fact free to question all those beliefs and values, but most of us do not. We may have been rebellious teenagers or even thought that we were great philosophers during our youth, but for most of us the core values we learnt during childhood are those that we believe in or return to.

There is comfort in what we know and are familiar with. Conversely, there is discomfort with that which is strange and unfamiliar. So we drift through school and maybe higher education. We certainly think about our occupation and probably

11

plan for it. Even here we may do so only within the limitations of our background, underestimating our abilities and so therefore not aiming high enough. Alternatively, we may conform to our parents' or society's expectations. For example, a bright student may be urged to go into the professions and be congratulated on so doing though they would really have preferred to do something else, something which may not have fitted the parental perception of success, but which would have given them a sense of adventure or greater fulfillment.

Whatever stage we are at in life, we can always pause for a moment and look at where we are. We can look at the alternatives, we can be eclectic and choose from the best that life has to offer and make our own decisions.

Put most simply, we can set our own course.

Mahatma Ghandi said: "*As human beings, our greatness lies, not so much in being able to remake the world, as in being able to remake ourselves.*"

Whatever circumstances we find ourselves in, we always have the choice of how to react to them. We can choose whether to find something positive in any situation. We can choose whether to be cheerful and whether or not to be happy.

In one company I worked for there was a constant turnover of staff occupying one particular position. The "maintenance" man, who also delivered the mail and acted as a driver, was often the butt of jokes. He was regarded as being rather strange and usually a bit lazy, always slinking around the office or hiding away in his basement lair.

Then Grant arrived. He was permanently genuinely cheerful. He obviously tried to do the best job he possibly could. In fact, his cheerfulness was infectious. When he went into the offices to deliver, collect or fix something he went in with a smile on his face. If appropriate, he said something and so interacted in some small way with all the people with whom he came into contact. Soon everyone knew his name; soon everyone's attitude to the mailman changed. People enjoyed Grant's visits, even the Chief

Executive chatted to Grant and had admiration for his ability to remain calm and cheerful.

The job was the same as it had been for all the other "mailmen," so what made Grant different? His home life was not unusual. He had a small house with a sizable mortgage. His wife worked at the local supermarket and his two teenage children were at times unpredictable and difficult.

Grant was not an abnormally good person. He was just an ordinary man living in the real world who chose to concentrate on the positive things. He was really proud of the fact that he owned his own home, something that his parents had never done. He did the best he could for his wife and she did the same for him. When his children were problematic, he remembered his own teenage years, when the hormones were flooding through him, and life was full of the uncertainty and angst of youth.

We all have the choice of reacting to life as Grant does, or we can choose not to. We all have the choice of living in a state of happiness, or we can allow ourselves to dwell on the negative and therefore choose not to be happy.

Many of us think of happiness as a time when we are feeling elated. Conversely, we think of ourselves as being sad when we feel depressed. Most of our lives are lived in the middle of the spectrum somewhere between these two states. What we can do is ensure that, through our attitude, our lives are predominantly lived at the warmer end of the spectrum. When we are sad or melancholic, we have to realize and value that this is part of life's richness, and that it is through this contrast that we can appreciate happiness when we experience it.

At this stage, we should not confuse happiness and success. H. Jackson Brown said: *"Success is getting what you want and happiness is liking what you get."* My own feeling is that we do, in fact, need to have some success. By that I do not mean that we have to be rich and powerful but we do need to feel that we have achieved some of our goals and that we have some influence over the events in our lives.

WHERE DO YOU WISH TO GET TO?

If we want the satisfaction of being fulfilled, we have to find our own path to fulfilment. Psychiatrists say that their job is solely to help some people function within society, not specifically to make them happy. We can only choose from different paths if we have an idea of our ultimate destination.

If we wish to lead a happy and fulfilling life, what questions can we ask ourselves? The first one is, "What makes me feel happy and fulfilled?"

Many people have never really considered this. In fact, they may answer without giving the question any real thought. They may well be too flippant and get the answer wrong. They may, for example, say something like: "A new car would make me happy," or "a relationship is what I want," whereas in reality having more friends or a balance to their work/life ratio may be what, deep down, they really want.

As we saw earlier, Maslow describes a hierarchy of needs through which he believes we all wish to progress. Unless we are in the most desperate situation, most of us are working at different levels at the same time.

We partially achieve some of our goals, such as our sense of security, while at the same time finding ways in which to socialise.

So the first thing is to take stock of where we are and then identify where we wish to be. Bearing in mind that we were all conditioned within the confines of our own family circumstance, what issues should we look at? Specifically, what questions could we ask ourselves to determine what we really want and how to get it?

Here are some questions to get us started.

What is my attitude to food?
How healthy is my diet?
How physically fit am I?
Would I like to be fitter?
Do I use alcohol in an acceptable way?
Do I use or abuse drugs?

Do I have enough money for my needs?
Do I like the work I do?

Am I under stress?
Do I feel that I contribute to society in some way?
Do I give "of myself" in any way?
Do I exercise choice in my life?
Do I have any behavioural patterns that I would like to change?

Am I in control of my emotions?
Am I optimistic?
Do I keep my problems in perspective?
Do I have people I can turn to if I need support?
Would I be willing to seek professional advice for emotional issues?

Do I like the person that I am?
Do I feel I get enough recognition in life?

Are there people I should forgive or from whom I should seek forgiveness?
What changes would I like to make in my life?
Am I grateful for the good things in my life?

Is there enough love in my life?
Do I have a good social life?
Do I have the sort of relationships I would like?
Do I have fun?

Is there enough laughter in my life?
Do I participate in enjoyable recreational activities?

What are my religious or spiritual beliefs?
Am I comfortable with these beliefs?

What is my attitude to sex?
Is that in harmony with what I practise?
What are my own moral values?
Do I honour my own values?
Am I honest with myself in understanding my own motivation for doing things?
Is my conscience clear?
What is the state of my mental health?

Of all these questions, I believe that the last is the most important.

OUR MENTAL HEALTH

Our own happiness and our ability to contribute to the lives of other people and society in general are all tied to our own mental health. There are also proven links between our mental and physical health. It is known that one can affect the other, but the key is mental health. As the great physician Socrates said over two thousand years ago, "*So neither ought you to attempt to cure the body without the soul.*"

Why is it that we fully understand the concept of keeping our bodies fit through exercise and diet but give little consideration to proactively increasing our mental fitness? Just as no-one is 100% physically fit, no-one is 100% mentally fit. Mental fitness is subjective anyway, so it is harder to define than physical fitness. But we can greatly increase our own level of mental fitness in accordance with what we consider to be desirable. It does, however, require the same thing as physical fitness – that is, a desire to become more fit and utilise self-discipline and appropriate knowledge to engage in a suitable fitness programme.

I was loathe to use the words "self-discipline" because, for most of us, this has connotations of hard work and doing things we do not wish to do. In this case, however, we set our own agenda for doing what we want, doing what makes us feel better. Surely all of us must welcome that.

When we plan a physical exercise programme we usually decide in advance what our goal is. We may wish to increase our aerobic capacity or develop a beautiful flat abdomen. What would be a suitable target for a mental health programme? For me, this would include the following:

- A sense of self-worth.

- A feeling that I have some control

- A belief that I can cope with most situations in life

- A feeling that I can make friends and socialise.

- A sense of optimism

- A belief that I am loveable

- A belief that I can give and receive love

- An ability to keep things in perspective

- An ability to laugh and have fun

- An ability to be flexible

SELF-WORTH / SELF-ESTEEM

Let's start with the concept of self-worth or, to use the phrase most of us are familiar with, our level of self-esteem. Before we can even look at this element, we have to look at the bigger picture of self-identity, of how we see ourselves.

This includes our gender, ethnic background, national affiliation, religious upbringing, socio-economic and educational background. We then add our physical appearance and age to this before going on to the less tangible questions of confidence and social ability. Most of us never really think about our identity. We just accept that we are who we are.

There are some aspects of ourselves which we cannot change. For example, the colour of our skin, our height or other physical features which are genetically determined. As we cannot change these facts about ourselves, it is to our own advantage to learn how to live with them as comfortably as possible. To worry about physical features over which we have no control is certainly understandable, but at the same time it can cause a debilitating drain on our emotional energy.

But the good news is that we do have the ability to change most other aspects of our lives. And it is the "other aspects" which give us the capacity for happy and fulfilling lives.

The Serenity Prayer by Reinhold Neibuhr sums this up pretty well:

"Grant me the serenity to accept the things I cannot change,
The courage to change the things that I can,
And the wisdom to know the difference."

Now let us now return to the concept of self-worth. This book will deal with many subjects relating to our sense of self-worth. All the subjects dealt with in this book, whether they are about money or relationships, affect our sense of self-worth, which in turn affects our overall sense of wellbeing and happiness.

We still live with many of the beliefs that our parents gave us. We emerge from childhood with certain attitudes, some of which are positive and beneficial and some of which are negative and constraining. We learnt most of our social skills from our parents. If they were cheerful and relaxed, so may we be. If they were negative and uptight, that is probably how we were and maybe still are.

The society in which we grow up and the affluence level of our families have a direct impact on our socialisation. In North America and much of Europe, parents try to give each child a bedroom of their own. In a religious studies class in Los Angeles, a small boy said that if Cain and Abel had been given separate bedrooms there would have been no murder. This boy said that he and his brother had separate bedrooms and that this system worked for them. In comparison, families in West Africa would consider it sad and cruel to isolate a child from the close companionship of their siblings. The use of social space and the expectation of how we will interact with other people is learnt in childhood.

As a small boy during the Second World War, the author J. G. Ballard was imprisoned by the Japanese in Shanghai. In his book, "Miracles of Life," he says: "*For the first time in my life, I was extremely close to my parents. At home we had our own bedrooms and bathrooms. I had never seen my parents naked or in bed together. Now I slept, ate, read, dressed and undressed within a few feet of them in the same small room. I revelled in this closeness. Lying in bed at night, I could, if I wanted to, reach out and take my mother's hand, though I never did.*"

Interestingly, Ballard's traumatic and chaotic childhood led him to become a psychiatrist. He, like all psychiatrists, psychotherapists and indeed all of us who are interested in personal growth always know who our first patient will be. It is ourselves.

Our sense of self-worth is the cornerstone on which our entire personality is built. What we think of ourselves is who we are. The process of learning about ourselves starts the day we are born and we have no control over it. As babies and young children, we receive character-developing recognition from other people. A mother is, of course, central to our lives and her relationship with us is paramount.

A friend of mine had an enviable childhood with an all-loving totally non-critical mother, hence she retains to this day the belief that she is naturally lovable. As a family, they talked and laughed a lot together. The children were made to feel included and worthwhile, which in turn gave them the gift of being sociable and having the natural ability to enjoy other people's company.

Another friend was always seen by his mother as an annoyance. He had interrupted the carefree flow of her busy working and social life. To this day, he sees himself as unwanted and, by extension, as an impediment in the lives of others.

Perhaps if those babies had been switched at birth they would also have switched ideas of their self-worth. How we start off in life is something over which we have no control, and as time passes the situation does not get much better. If we enter kindergarten feeling loved it will affect our ability to socialise and interact with other children, although even this is not straightforward. A much loved child may be selfish and in turn upset other children, while an unloved child could either be withdrawn or become over-accommodating to compensate.

Whatever the situation, it is the start of a lifelong process in which we come to see ourselves as being a particular type of person. We adapt and tend to reinforce the personality type we think we are.

The very day after I started writing this section of the book, I witnessed a classic example of how a child's self-image was being formed, or rather malformed. At a busy crossroads I noticed a mother several steps ahead of her small son, who in turn was pushing a child's buggy in which there was a still younger boy. When the mother was halfway across the road, a large vehicle, which was being driven too quickly, started to make a turn into the road they were crossing. The young boy, whose view was partially obscured by a parked vehicle, did the right thing and pulled back onto the pavement. He had made a quick judgment and used his commonsense to protect his younger brother and himself.

Instead of being congratulated on his quick thinking, his mother, who was by now already on the other side of the road, annoyed by his apparent slowness and perhaps feeling somewhat guilty at her own lack of care, screamed at him, "*You stupid boy. You stupid, stupid boy.*" So many people sadly suffer throughout their lives, even into old age, from the damage resulting from such poor judgment from their parents, their teachers and their peers.

The adjectives most often used to describe us reinforce who we think we are – lovable, disruptive, fun, aggressive, cheerful, obnoxious, happy, sad and stupid. The more we hear these words said about us the more we live up to those expectations of ourselves. A study in America followed young children through a typical day. It was found that, on average, each child was exposed to 92 negative comments and 16 positive ones. In short, adults admonish children far more frequently than we praise them – over five criticisms for every positive comment.

Criticising our children seems to be a universal theme throughout time. Dr Robert Darwin wrote a letter to his son Charles, when the latter was at Cambridge supposedly studying theology. The letter said, "*You care for nothing but shooting dogs and rat catching and you will be a disgrace to yourself and to your family.*"

Walking with a friend in a public park, she told me that she felt very much like one of the closely clipped yew hedges we could see. All her natural instincts to grow exuberantly outwards and upwards had been cut back. She had been trained into rigid conformity. It reminded me of the pertinent question one character asks in a play by Philip Roth, "*Where did you get the idea that the most wonderful thing that I could be in life was obedient?*"

Over-protective parents can unintentionally damage their children. Making adult decisions about everything on behalf of their offspring means that children never learn to make decisions for themselves. It is much better to give a child some freedom and teach them to make decisions. It can be a simple matter such as saying, "Which T-shirt would you like to wear today? The yellow one or the blue one?"

Shielding and protecting our children from physical harm and emotional difficulty prevents them from going through the natural learning process of maturing. The paradox is that over-caring and over-supportive parents can produce children who are not adequately trained and prepared for the vicissitudes of adult life: people who cannot take responsibility, people who are not used to organising their own finances, and people unable to form equal relationships because they are constantly looking for parental figures who will look after them.

One caring primary school teacher tries very hard to encourage, rather than criticize, her class. For example, a small boy was slopping water from a painting jar as he walked across the classroom. She calmly said to him "Peter, if you hold the jar with both hands and walk very slowly you will be able to take it across the room without spilling another drop." Her philosophy is to correct the action, not criticize the child. According to Alan H. Hanaline, "*Motivation is a matter of helping people to do things by and for themselves without threatening or belittling as they go about their efforts.*"[1]

By the time we reach our teenage years, our place in society has pretty well been established. We know how we fit in, or not,

1. *Training in Business and Industry*, Gellert Publishing

and we know our strengths and weaknesses. We know the areas in which we succeed and those in which we fail.

The problem is that most of us accept this situation as being final. It is not. Where we are at any stage of life is where circumstance has brought us. We have the capacity to change the way things will be in the future. We can look at the various facets of our lives and adjust them to how we want them to be. We can do this by focusing on them one by one and then making changes which lead us in the direction in which we truly wish to go. In terms of character, we can become the person we wish to be.

Building our sense of self-worth is the best place to start. When asked who is responsible for children's self-esteem, 96% of all teachers surveyed said it was the parents. More surprisingly, when asked the same question, 94% of all parents said that it was the teachers' responsibility.

In adulthood, we are all responsible for our own self-esteem. The greatest gift we can give ourselves is the belief that we are worthy and capable of happiness and success. Let me repeat that. *Worthy and capable of happiness and success.* This is the core belief which gives us self-esteem.

So why do we not all have it? We all have a version of it as babies. We uninhibitedly cried loudly, demanded what we wanted, which was to be fed and to be held. But in time we are taught that this is inappropriate behaviour for older children to use. We are understandably sanctioned and criticised in order to curb our natural inclinations. We cannot have a society in which all adults think only of themselves and scream loudly for everything they want.

The key issue then is the most difficult one. How do parents transform their offspring into socially well adjusted children and young adults? In an ideal world, children would learn to drop childish ways and adopt a balanced, realistic and positive way of interacting with the world around them. In most cases, however, this does not happen smoothly. One of the reasons is that our parents were not perfect themselves. We are unintentionally misguided by them, just as they in turn were unintentionally misguided by their parents.

So the fact is that, in most cases, we have been taught things which are not beneficial to our own sense of entitlement to be happy and successful. To a greater or lesser extent, everyone has some negative feelings in their psychological background. Moreover, it is often our perception which is more important and damaging than reality.

In his play, A Woman of No Importance, Oscar Wilde said:

"Children begin by loving their parents; after a time they judge them; rarely, if ever, do they forgive them."

The poet Philip Larkin was less eloquent but more direct in his criticism of the parental process when he wrote: "*They fuck you up, your Mum and Dad.*"

For whatever reason, most of us need to change many of our self-beliefs. This can be done and this book will give some guidance as to how it can be done. What is needed is a desire to embrace a greater sense of peace within ourselves and a determination to change. As importantly, we need to decide for ourselves what aspects of our personality and self-beliefs we wish to change.

DO I LIKE THE PERSON I AM?

A six year old boy once said *"When someone loves you, the way they say your name is different. You just know that your name is safe in their mouth."*

Our name is always important to us. It was the name chosen specifically for us, usually by our parents. Whether or not we like our name or are dissatisfied with it, is often an indication of how we feel about ourselves. If at any stage of life someone chooses to be known by another name, it is usually indicative of a strong desire to change the person they are into the person they wish to be.

The degree to which we like or dislike someone ranges through the full spectrum. In extreme cases, we may feel that someone is worthy of our total love and respect or, alternatively, that someone is obnoxious and loathsome. Usually, we take a more balanced view, recognising the composite mix of qualities and characteristics which form most personalities.

We know ourselves far better than we know anybody else. We look at our own characteristics and make exactly the same judgments, although sometimes we can be more critical of ourselves than we are of other people. If, on balance, we are happy with what we see, we have a level of self-liking or self-respect. If we are not happy with what we see, we lack self-respect, which in turn may leave us feeling that we do not like the person we are.

It is both desirable and important that we should like and respect ourselves. This should not be confused with conceit and arrogance, which are often attributable to an overall sense of insecurity. It boils down to the fact that liking ourselves and having self-respect is the foundation on which a healthy personality is built. If we do not like the person we are, it must surely be impossible to find happiness. So how can we develop self-liking?

The first thing is to think about our own personality. What characteristics do we have that we like, and what characteristics do we find objectionable? We should take pleasure in recognising own positive characteristics and then develop a plan to change the negative ones.

For example, we might have a personality trait such as rudeness, intolerance, selfishness or dishonesty. If we genuinely wish to change one of these traits, it is probably a good idea to study it in more detail in order to understand how it manifests itself.

A rude or short-tempered person may come to understand that they react in this way when they feel frustrated. They could then look at the situations in which they are likely to become frustrated. The next step is to plan in advance how to react on future occasions when there is the potential for frustration and the consequent rudeness. This is easier to do when we understand that we are going to modify our behaviour for our own benefit.

If we do decide to make changes, we can plan the best way in which to make these changes. It would be far too large a task to change several personality characteristics at one time. So, like any project, it is worth taking one aspect at a time, planning it carefully and then proceeding.

Most of us expend a lot of energy trying to win the approval of other people. This may be to convince ourselves that if other people approve of us, we have worthwhile qualities about which we ourselves are uncertain. We make the mistake of basing our own sense of worth on other people's criteria and valuations. My suggestion is that we should all seek the approval of the person who matters to us most. That is ourselves.

The overall goal is to become a person we ourselves like and respect. The confidence this gives us usually means that other people reflect our self-evaluation and accept us in this way as well.

DEVELOPING SELF-RESPECT

I prefer the term self-respect to self-esteem. First of all, because the word esteem is somewhat old-fashioned and, secondly, because basic respect, as opposed to elevated esteem, is all that we require of our self image to function in a happy, positive way.

If we have respect for another person, that is a way of saying that we find them and their actions acceptable, or at least some aspects of them or their actions. So for us to have self-respect, we must also find some of our own actions acceptable. Our actions include our thoughts, the things we say, and our physical manner. Remember, we are not aiming for perfection. No one is perfect. But while we acknowledge our imperfections, the key is to recognise and celebrate those qualities within ourselves which are worthwhile.

We cannot change or improve a situation unless we are fully aware of exactly what the situation is. Therefore, a good starting point is to take a look at how we currently see ourselves. What is our self assessment? How do we currently identify ourselves? This includes gender, ethnic background, national and religious affiliation, socio-economic and educational background. We then add to this our physical appearance and age, before going onto the less tangible questions of confidence and social ability.

Most of us never really think about our identities. We are what we are. We are comfortable with people who are similar to ourselves and increasingly less at ease with people whose background is increasingly divergent from our own. But this is a time to think about our identities. This is the time to ask ourselves if we are happy with our role and place in society. We should ask ourselves what kind of person do we wish to become?

This is the time to start thinking positively. Ask yourself what you do like about yourself. It can be any one of a thousand different qualities. Your gentleness, your strength, your willingness to give, your kindness, your cleverness, your modesty. These are all commendable qualities. You may have others such as a strong vocational or educational background. Or even a love of music or some other recreational activity. Whatever the answer is, it is now important to build on this feeling. Self-respect must grow from within.

Take this germ of an idea and build on it. Look at this positive aspect of yourself and recognise that this is a quality which you respect. A quality which gives you self-respect and can be used as the starting point to build a portfolio of positive concepts about yourself. These in turn will provide a strong foundation for self-respect.

At this stage, it is very important to avoid negative thoughts and harmful comparisons. For example, you could take pride in the fact that you are going to a gym on a regular basis. You could rightly have self-respect for maintaining this self-discipline. You could rightly have self-respect for the effort you expend every time you go to the gym. You could rightly have self-respect for the progress that you are making at the gym.

Do not in any way damage the self-respect you are building by comparing yourself with other people in the gym or in any other way. Other people's ability is not the issue. Unless you are entering a competition, your only concern should be your own level of growth and achievement. If we fall into the trap of comparison with others, we will almost certainly lose. The chances are that there will always be someone, possibly many people, who are physically stronger than ourselves, intellectually superior or are more gifted in some special way. It is also worth remembering that all of us are good at some things and less good at others. Just because somebody is physically stronger than us does not indicate anything other than the fact that on one measurement scale they have some advantages.

Dr Paul Hauk says in his excellent book, "Hold Your Head Up High", that comparison with others is the pivotal issue concerning a sense of self-worth. He rightly says that if we never compare ourselves with other people, we will never damage our self-opinion. The problem with this is that on many occasions in life we are in a competitive situation. For example, when we are applying for a job, it is highly probable that there will be more than one candidate. In such circumstances, we know that we will be compared with other people. The difficult but important thing to remember is that our feelings of self-worth should not be affected by this.

The key issue is what we think of ourselves. Let us be realistic and recognise in ourselves the qualities which we like and the efforts we are making to strengthen and build on those. Human nature is such that we all like to receive compliments and all feel the sting of criticism. To build our sense of self-worth, we must avoid the necessity of relying on other people's approval and, equally, we must avoid the pitfall of oversensitivity to negative comments.

That is not to say that we should not enjoy compliments when we receive them. It is a very healthy sign not only to receive compliments but also to have the maturity to accept them in a genuine and open way. Similarly, there will be many occasions when we cannot stop other people from criticising us. We can, however, decide how we react to such criticism. We will preferably look for the truth in any criticism and act appropriately rather than over-reacting, such as losing our temper and denying any culpability.

Building self-respect cannot be done instantly. When my nephew went to a new, all-boys school, at the age of 13, he felt very nervous. Many of the boys already at the school were, in fact young men of 17 or 18. They were physically strong and had a level of confidence which had been built up over the preceding few years.

The headmaster of the school called a meeting at which he

addressed all the new boys. He told them that nobody in this school was going to give them any respect. He did say, however, that they could earn as much respect as they wanted. They could earn that respect in the way that they conducted themselves in the school.

Specifically, they had to learn how to live in a society made up of the other boys and the staff. They had to learn how to deal with the pressures and the pleasures which came from living in close proximity with so many other people. They had to learn to cope with the various circumstances that life would throw at them each day. They had to cope with the unfairness and injustice they would encounter. This was after all, no more than a microcosm of the world outside, with all of its attendant unfairness and inequalities.

They could earn the respect of their peers by the way in which they handled themselves. The key was not what other people did to them but how they reacted was what mattered. Being knocked down in a rugby tackle was no disgrace, but avoiding that tackle could lose the respect of their fellow team members and in turn their own self-respect.

Everyone could not be top of the class, said the headmaster, but they could all work to the best of their ability. So long as they gave real effort to their studies, they would gain and keep the respect of their fellow students and teachers. The main thing was not to give in, whether it was in their studies, on the playing fields or in their dealings with other people. Always strive to improve the situation and to make it better, always to set a realistic target and to keep aiming for it.

They were encouraged to find something that interested them. The subject was not particularly important. What was important was the benefit that they would receive from focusing on something which was special to them. There's a saying that "*our energy flows where our attention goes.*"

By focusing on something, it is probable that they could get to know quite a lot about it. To take an easy example, they could become really keen on a sport such as soccer. That does not mean that they have to play it themselves but it does mean that they appreciate the talent of others. It gives a mutual interest with other people and something about which they can talk interestingly and knowledgeably.

Their special focus could be on computers, music, space travel or anything else. Whatever it is, they could build their own self respect in the sure knowledge that they know a lot about that particular subject and gain pleasure from it.

The headmaster then quoted Thomas Carlyle who said, *"Nothing builds self-esteem and self-confidence like accomplishment."* I would add to this the quality of human resilience and reiterate that as we get older our level of self-confidence is more and more a matter that we ourselves can deliberately improve and control.

As always, William Shakespeare summed up self-respect more concisely than anyone else when he said:

"This above all: To thine own self be true, and it must follow, as the night of the day, thou canst not then be false to any man."

SELF-CONFIDENCE

The word confidence traces its roots to the Latin verb "fidere," which means "to trust." So, self-confidence means trusting in ourselves.

If we conducted a survey and asked people what personality trait they would most like to have, I am sure that many people would reply self-confidence.

If we then asked them to give an example of someone with self-confidence, they would probably come up with a name like James Bond. He is a man who can face the most dangerous and impossible situations in the sure belief that he will succeed. As this is fantasy, he will succeed whether it is escaping from the jaws of death, winning at the roulette table or proving to be completely irresistible to all women.

In real life, there are many people who are confident and successful. Yet even the most powerful have a degree of self-doubt. Winston Churchill, at the height of his power, poured out his feelings of despondency to his daughter-in-law, Pamela Harriman. No one is confident and successful 100% of the time. What confident people all share is a belief, based on the evidence at hand, that they are likely to succeed. This results from their track record of past success. What builds confidence is trial and error. They have made mistakes and there have been times, possibly many times, when they have not succeeded. What they have done, however, is learn from their mistakes. These mistakes have not stopped them from proceeding but have simply given them the guidance to do things differently, to do things in a way which is more likely to succeed.

As Peter McIntyre said, "*Confidence comes from not always being right but from not fearing to be wrong.*"

We can all have confidence but we will not have total confidence in every situation. Let me give you an example. Some years ago a successful New York lawyer who exuded confidence was visiting a friend in Oregon. He was driving in a remote area to what his friend referred to as a fishing cabin when his car broke down. As time passed and no-one came by, he became more concerned that he might have to spend the night in his car.

Finally, an ancient pick-up truck could be heard and then seen as it came round a bend on the gravel road. The driver was a local man who was the complete opposite of the lawyer. He struggled to find seasonal employment in the nearby sawmill and lived modestly in that remote area because that was all he had ever known. He had always avoided the city people who came out to their wonderful summer houses which they dismissively referred to as "cabins." Circumstances had, however, now brought these two men together. As darkness fell, the lawyer was increasingly nervous and ill at ease. The lumberman, however, was not only on his home territory but had been fixing cars all his life. Who do you think felt more confident in this situation?

We all have confidence in certain things and under certain circumstances. The next step is to develop a strategy to build on the confidence we already have. Let us say, for example, that we lack confidence in our ability to meet new people and to socialise. The important thing here is that we have identified the problem. Now let's rephrase this in the form of a goal we would like to achieve. It could be, "I would like to have the ability to go into a group of people whom I do not know and chat comfortably with them." Great! We have now set a target. Importantly, this target is realistic and completely achievable.

The best way to begin is by asking, "What is now stopping me from doing this"? The answer may well be a fear of rejection. The idea that the group we are entering will not want us. The idea that we do not have anything of value to offer those people.

Now let's take this reasoning a step further. If we were going into a meeting of Nobel physicists and we know nothing about physics, this may well be true. Especially if we pretend to know something about the subjects they are discussing. Similarly, if we go to a football club and have no interest in football, we are probably not going to find it easy to integrate.

Logically, however, there will be no reason for us to go to an event which is not relevant to us in some way. In order to go to a party or meeting, we must have been invited or there must be some form of open invitation which included us. So the first thing to remember is that we do have a right to be there. In fact, we have just as much right to be there as anyone else.

One situation, which could potentially cause us to be nervous, is going into a group in which many people already know each other. We then have a choice of how we react to this. We can feel scared and think of ourselves as an outsider. Or we can think more positively. We can say to ourselves, "these people will be interested in meeting someone new." If people are chatting in little groups, it could well be because they know the other people well and feel comfortable in these groups. It is also possible that they need the security of being part of a group. In other words, they might like to chat to you but do not themselves have the social skills to come over and speak with you.

How we handle ourselves in a situation like this is important. If we are shy and remain on our own at the side of the room, other people will observe and subconsciously note the shyness. People will believe of us what we believe of ourselves. Alternatively, if we have the courage and determination to go up and speak to someone, we will have achieved many things. Most practically, we will have found a starting point. The subconscious antennae of the other people present will see us as someone who has integrated easily. More important still is the fact that we will see ourselves as someone who has quickly integrated. In doing this, we are taking the first positive step towards becoming socially confident.

If you are saying to yourself, "That is too great a step for me, I just simply could not do that," you are already setting yourself up for failure rather than success. Making progress does require courage, determination and effort. One piece of advice that might help is the old adage, "Fake it 'til you make it." What this means is that you simply act as if you have the skills and confidence that you would like to have.

Similarly, we should never imagine or visualise any scenario other than that which we wish to see happen. If we think and act positively often enough those skills become reality. Conversely, if we consistently act in an inappropriate way or dwell on failure, that too becomes reality. The choice is ours.

Yes, the choice is ours. The choice about how we behave in any situation in which we have freedom is ours, and we always have freedom in how we think.

Given time and effort, we can build a level of confidence in any aspect of our lives. If we wish to be confident in our ability to physically defend ourselves, we can build up our skills in that area by taking the appropriate training and keeping ourselves fit. If we want to mix easily with other people, we can practise this by going into new groups and developing these skills. If we wish to have the confidence to speak in public, we can develop these skills by joining a supportive organisation such as Toastmasters International.

The public speaking organisation "Toastmasters International" is a very good example of how confidence can and should be built. When a visitor comes to a club for the first time, anywhere in the world, they are made to feel welcome. They are immediately put at their ease and told that they will not be required to do anything which they do not wish to do. They are assured that they will not have to give any type of speech. The newcomer can simply observe what other people do and see if this sort of thing is of interest to them.

As with any organisation, there must have been some basic interest or need which drew someone to attend. In the case of a speakers club, it may be that they have to give presentations at work. It could be that they have to prepare for a specific speaking engagement such as giving a "best man's" speech. It could be that they wish to find a forum in which they can express themselves. Or it could simply be that this is a wonderful way in which to overcome shyness, build self-confidence and meet interesting people.

Whatever the reason they are there, they will be brought into a system in which they make gradual progress. When they feel comfortable with what happens in the meeting, they may be asked if they would like to fill a simple role such as that of timekeeper. This requires only that they record times and, at some stage, read them out in front of the other club members. This is the first simple step towards being in front of a group. The new club member then takes a series of small steps, each step building on the experience and confidence gained before. In this way, people make progress at their own speed.

Like any other skill, some people will work harder at it and pursue it more than others. So some people will develop greater skills at public speaking. The point is that everyone will make continual progress. Everyone will develop a sense of confidence that they did not have before and confidence is like a muscle – the more you exercise it the stronger it becomes.

If we use the same format of a gentle introduction followed by steady growth in ability, we can develop a level of confidence in anything we want to. We can choose to be confident in anything we wish.

Does the size of the task scare you off? For example, you may like the idea of playing tennis at your local tennis club, but in the past have only played a little tennis and know that you are not particularly fit. The jump from being virtually unable to play to becoming a reasonable club player seems enormous. Alternatively, if you wish to graduate from university but have not completed high school, the leap may appear to be impossibly large. It is the same with any other large project. If you look only at the enormity of the undertaking and dwell on the hard work and problems that face you, it is more than likely that you will give up in despair.

I am always amazed at the ability human beings have to undertake massive engineering projects. Skyscraper buildings, mile long bridges and motorway networks which, quite literally, change the shape of the earth. Yet all of these great undertakings were achieved in the same way. The project, which started as an idea or as someone's vision, was considered to be worthwhile and then planned as a sequence of actions. Most importantly, a proposed critical path was laid out, so that the engineers who worked on these projects were fully aware of just how much time and effort was to be expended. They knew that they would encounter difficulties and that unforeseen problems would arise, yet they still went ahead.

On an individual basis, we must be just as proactive. We must decide what is important to us and plan appropriately. The would-be tennis player can start by making enquiries about club membership. At the same time, they can commence a mild program of exercise, such as walking on a daily basis. They could start taking tennis lessons and develop the basic skills needed to play at the club. The logical thing would be to get to know other new club members and begin playing with people who were also new to the game. In this way, ability and confidence would grow together.

The student who wishes to complete a university degree should first decide why they wish to do this. Is it because they need a degree in order to pursue their career, or is it because they simply wish to learn about new things? In both cases, they will have to break it down into manageable sections. The first will be to complete any educational requirements for university entrance. This in itself may well require dedication and hard work. When enrolled at university, a student has to think in two parallel ways: long-term he or she has the target of completing all the requirements for a degree; short-term the aim is to complete each course and slowly build up to the number of credits that are needed.

Many years ago, when we lived in Canada and our children were young, we wanted to have a place in the country where our children could run around out of doors in the fresh air. A place devoid of television, where we could play games and just enjoy being a family together.

My wife and I spent a lot of time looking at the various options. What we wanted and what we could afford were two very different things. We wanted a beautiful waterfront cottage with lovely views. This in turn had to be within a reasonable driving distance of the city. We did not actually have any money sitting in the bank, so whatever we did would require borrowing.

Was the whole idea worth getting into debt? Given that we were young, we felt that it was. We would have the benefit of the cottage at the time of life when it was most appropriate for our family. But that still did not mean that we should be foolhardy. We could not simply decide to borrow what for us were large amounts of money without any plan as to how we would repay it. After all, this was designed to improve the quality of our lives, not to add the worry of unmanageable debt.

After looking at numerous properties such as abandoned farms, dilapidated summer homes and various plots of land, we decided on the latter. We purchased a west-facing water front lot on a lake, two hours drive north of the city in which we lived. It was a lake we already knew quite well because we had camped there on several occasions.

This was really exciting. We, or more precisely the bank, then owned a lovely little piece of densely wooded land on a beautiful lake. We spent several weekends camping on the gravel track close to the plot, planning and visualising what we wanted. We then drew up a sequence of what needed to be done. An entrance driveway needed to be cleared and built. About fifty of the tightly packed Aspen trees needed to be cut down in order to open up a building site. The stumps of these trees then had to be removed and after all that it would be possible to build the cabin.

In order to keep costs down, it was my intention to do as

much of the work as possible. I could and did cut down all of the trees but had to bring in a bulldozer to clear the stumps and level the plot. I took "hands on" evening courses in timber frame construction. This in turn allowed me to design and build a single storey, three-bedroom, two-bathroom cottage.

When I needed the help of other people, I decided to do what the first pioneers had always done in the West – hold a "barn raising" event. In my case, I sent out formal invitation cards to many of my friends. On the front page it read, "You are Invited to an Erection Party." Most of them enjoyed the joke as well as the weekend in which we raised the walls.

At the end, we had more or less what we wanted – a comfortable, reasonably spacious family retreat with a large deck from which we could watch the sun setting over the lake. I described the building process in little more than a couple of paragraphs. Looking back, I think of the achievement with great pride. But the reality was two years of very hard work and an endless series of problems and frustrations. Am I glad I did it? Yes, certainly. Was it worth all the effort? Yes, it was.

Getting what we want is not easy. It requires enormous motivation. It may also require the taking of risks, but if there is something that we really want strongly enough, there is a strong possibility that it can be achieved. Especially if we break the project down into manageable sections and give ourselves the reward of seeing small individual goals achieved and overall progress being made.

Remember the saying, "*Yard by yard is hard, but inch by inch is a cinch.*" And of course, a mile is no more than a succession of inches.

In the following pages, we will look at a range of individual issues, one by one, which help build our sense of self-respect. We will do this by looking at life issues which affect all of us as human beings. We can then make a conscious decision about what we believe, what we value and what we aspire to in our lives.

Just like taking a degree or building a cottage, we should look at each of the stages as a project in itself. We should focus on those issues which have priority for us at the time, and we should take pleasure as we make progress and achieve our goals in each of these steps. In this case, our goal should be to develop confidence, devoid of arrogance.

Having considered the foundations, let's consider each "level" in turn.

LEVELS 1 & 2

BASIC LIFE NEEDS FOR SURVIVAL

BIOLOGICAL/PHYSIOLOGICAL AND SAFETY NEEDS

The base level of Abraham Maslow's pyramid rightly identifies our requirement to satisfy our most basic needs of hunger, thirst, sleep and shelter. The second level identifies our need to feel protected, to feel safe and secure.

In its most rudimentary terms, the vast majority of people, and certainly anyone reading this book, would be assumed to have risen above these stages long ago. The reality for 21st century human beings is that we have to reinterpret these basic needs and elaborate on them.

For example, we do indeed need to have food and shelter, but as we are no longer hunter gatherers, our requirement is to have sufficient money to purchase these. Moreover, we still wish to feel physically safe which may mean that collectively we have to provide a security service, such as the police force, through the payment of taxes. By extension, our sense of security may well be tied to our how secure we feel in our employment or our ability to generate income.

We also wish to be safe from disease and injury. Therefore any activity we undertake or any food we ingest should be beneficial in some way and should not impair or shorten our lives. The following sections are an interpretation of our basic needs in the world in which we currently live.

PHYSICAL HEALTH

When we are young, the primary concern for most people about our bodies is that we should be attractive. The idea that some of our bodily functions will slowly deteriorate, or cease to work at all, seems unimaginable. With maturity, we realise that the world is full of illness and that with old age comes physical deterioration.

Athletes and people involved in sport are, of course competitive by nature. We understand that they train in special ways for their special needs. The rest of us, if we are sensible, will monitor our health in whatever way is necessary to remain fit and active. All of us want our bodies to function well. We want to be able to walk reasonable distances without becoming breathless. We want to be able to undertake the physical tasks required by day-to-day living. Just like our car, we expect our bodies to do what they are designed to do.

Most of us understand the basic concept of servicing a car. The oil has to be changed on a regular basis and various parts, such as brake pads, must be replaced. Maintenance becomes even more important for aircraft. Jet engines and all mechanical systems in aircraft are regularly checked and overhauled. When we think about the huge number of flights crossing the globe every day, it is amazing how few crashes take place and what a tiny percentage of those are caused by inadequate maintenance.

If, however, we were to analyse the causes of illness in any major hospital, we would find that a high percentage of the diseases are caused either by lack of maintenance or by actual abuse. People talk about having a heart attack or a stroke, which they say was "completely unexpected." For many of these patients, however, their situation would not be considered unexpected by medical professionals. The doctors treating them would consider that there was a statistical probability for people with certain lifestyles to develop those illnesses. The manual worker who stokes up on fried food clogging his arteries or a desk-bound city worker producing a constant, stress-related, flow of adrenaline. Both are at risk and both should be aware of the risks which they face.

Just as we can have long-term financial plans, so we can give some thought to long-term health.

Part of the problem is that many people, outside the medical profession, are genuinely unaware of the risks which surround them. We become slightly more aware when we travel. We understand that if we go to the tropics we may be at risk of contracting malaria. What we need is to be more conscious of diseases which are not caused by a single mosquito bite but are the result of our ongoing lifestyle.

As children, many of us wished we could see into the future. We would like to have known what career we would choose, whom we would marry, whether we would have children and how long we would live. Actually, being able to see into our personal future would be terrifying. For example, knowing for sure that we would spend our last few years in the pain and suffering caused by a terrible illness is not something that we wish to look forward to. In our unrealistic optimism, we assume that we will carry on with our current level of fitness and that at some stage in the distant future our lives will comfortably come to a close.

The reality we might (or might not) wish to consider is all those people in geriatric hospital wards. We should think about the "old folks" homes with numerous old people sitting around, many wearing incontinence pads, while their minds slowly deteriorate through lack of interest and lack of stimulus. We cannot control our health 100%. Nor can we yet control our genetic propensity to suffer from certain illnesses. We can, however, reduce the risk of developing many diseases through our lifestyle and we can choose to keep our bodies and minds as active as possible for as long as possible.

There was a large sign in a postnatal clinic, warning of childhood diseases, which read "*Are you aware that the first year of your life is the most dangerous?*" Graffiti scrawled across the bottom replied, "*Yes, but your last year is not without its hazards either!*"

Anyone responsible for children will always want to protect them against childhood diseases. The measles, mumps and rubella inoculation (MMR) has been highly controversial in the past few years. It is understandable that parents become undecided if they hear so-called experts expressing concerns over its safety. The problem that faces all of us as laymen is the vast amount of often conflicting information from which we try to make sense. Eventually we must make a decision and, prior to that, we must decide how much effort we are willing to put into weighing the pros and cons of such a decision.

Someone with two very healthy teenage sons says they never seem to get sick and even appear not to feel the cold. The amount of clothes they wear does not change much with the passing of the seasons. These two boys grew up in West Africa, which in colonial times was known as a place of "dysentery, danger and death" and "the white man's graveyard." The mother of these two boys has the theory that much of their good health is due to the fact that they were not pampered and closeted. They were constantly playing in the garden, examining insects and generally getting dirty. She attributes their good health to the natural immunity we can develop as children when not over-protected by too much soap and water.

We need to protect our bodies both internally and externally. The human body is a remarkably frail structure. If we slap a large man on the back we mistakenly think that this bulk is strong. It cannot, however, withstand most of the effects of gravity, not to mention many of the risks we take on a daily basis. Getting hit by a car or the physical dangers which are ever present in many occupational and recreational activities.

We only have to look at human remains from the past to see that by the time they died, many people had incurred major physical damage. Today in some developing countries where appalling work conditions are unregulated, we still see an unacceptably high occurrence of maiming and dismemberment.

Generally speaking, we are quite conscientious and sensible about protecting our physical body. Those who do have accidents sometimes know that they could have protected themselves, or even avoided the activity which was potentially dangerous. No one is suggesting that we should cease to play rugby or stop riding bicycles. Quite the opposite. What a boring place the world would become if we took no risks at all. Our choice comes into effect when we decide how much risk we are willing to take, and offset this against the convenience of riding a motor scooter or the thrill of white water rafting.

One of the most dramatic and frightening photographs ever taken is of a French climber. She uses no safety equipment at all, and in this picture is seen hanging by her fingers beneath a rocky over-ledge above a 600 foot drop. Interestingly, she says that not using any type of a security rope is safer for her than having one. She knows that she must always rely totally on herself alone. She also knows, every time she starts a climb, this could potentially be the last day of her life. For her, the excitement outweighs the possibility of losing her life.

AVOIDABLE ILLNESSES

Over 75% of all the illnesses and diseases from which we suffer are avoidable.

Riding a motorcycle does not mean that we will inevitably have an accident. It does, however, mean that statistically we are more likely to have a serious, or even fatal, accident than non-motorcycle riders. Even among motorcyclists there is a spectrum of risk taking, which in turn increases or reduces their chances of having an accident. Our choice of lifestyle puts us into, or removes us from, certain categories of risk and probable outcome.

Physical accidents are something that we can readily understand. From the school playground onwards we have seen people getting hurt and bleeding. Illness and disease may be something with which we are less familiar and so feel less threatened by. The sick are either in hospitals or hidden away at home. Most people only become aware of illness when it affects them or someone close to them. In some ways this is unfortunate because we cannot make sensible lifestyle choices if we do not know what the dangers are and cannot visualise the outcome.

If we describe the day-to-day lifestyle of a diabetic and outline the very serious potential health problems, then individuals can decide for themselves if they wish to modify their lifestyle accordingly. This section will outline some common diseases which can affect us, at all ages, but which are in many circumstances preventable.

Diabetes is a major cause of blindness, kidney disease, high blood pressure, heart disease and amputation of the lower legs and feet. On a daily basis, it requires that the sufferer takes from themselves, and tests, small blood samples. Depending on the type of diabetes, they then have to take oral medication or inject themselves with insulin. All diabetics must maintain strict control over their food intake and are substantially limited, not just by sugar, but also by foods such as white bread, which release their sugars into the bloodstream very quickly.

Some diabetics develop their condition as a result of heredity. Many, however, are responsible for causing their own diabetes. Type 2 diabetes can develop (or can be caused to develop) at any age but the risk does increase as we get older. Anyone from teenagers to adults, but especially those who are overweight and consume too much sugar, including soda drinks and sweets, are at risk. Reaching maturity gives a false sense of security. In the United States, one in five people aged between 65 and 75 is diabetic.

We can avoid developing lifestyle-induced type 2 diabetes by ensuring that we are not fat. A simple gauge of this is our waist measurement. Professor Anthony Barnett, in a BBC interview, said fat cells which develop around the waist pump out chemicals which damage the insulin system. *"Men with waists of more than 40 inches and women with waist measurements of more than 35 inches are at an incredibly high risk of type 2 diabetes and heart disease. Thicker waistlines may double to quadruple the risks of developing these diseases compared with people who have slimmer waistlines. Even a lower waist measurement of 37 inches in men and 32 inches in women may significantly raise the risk of both of these diseases."*

Dr Ian Campbell, of the National Obesity Forum said that *"People with large waists are just as much at risk of type 2 diabetes and heart disease as those who are clinically obese."* Simple recommendations concerning diet and exercise can be found here and in the next chapters.

Heart disease, a leading cause of death in the West, is a general term used for a variety of heart-related illnesses, all of which affect the heart's ability to work normally. Most common among these is coronary artery disease which occurs when the arteries (which supply blood to the heart) slowly become clogged with a sticky material called plaque. This has the effect of reducing the flow of blood to the heart which not only puts a strain on the heart but can, in time, cause a heart attack, which is the death of a part of the heart muscle.

The same conditions which are responsible for heart disease can also cause a **stroke**. That is when insufficient blood reaches a part of the brain causing the death of brain cells and a consequent lack of brain function. People who have had a stroke often suffer paralysis on one side of the body and may also have their speech affected.

The risk of developing heart disease or having a stroke can be reduced by lifestyle changes involving some obvious things, such as not smoking. We can also ensure that we keep our cholesterol level and blood pressure low through controlling what we eat and by taking some exercise.

Other people's **oral hygiene** is quickly apparent to us. The white teeth and pink gums of the young look healthy and attractive. Conversely, stained and uncared for teeth cause us to recoil in horror. Can you imagine anyone wanting to kiss such a mouth? Without consciously studying someone's teeth, we instantly get a sense of their colour, which do darken with age, and whether or not the teeth and gums look healthy. Bad breath may also be caused by bacteria within the mouth. More important still is that oral health, including the condition of the tongue, is often indicative of general health.

Let us also not forget that, like women's breasts, teeth are not there merely for ornamentation but have an important function. Our ability to consume and enjoy food is dependent on the health of our teeth and gums. With regular and careful maintenance we should be able to retain and use the majority of our teeth throughout our lives.

A few years ago I came home and listened to a rather unusual message on my answer-phone. It was a friend, and she said in a rather jokey way, "*Would you please let me have three large testicles and five small breasts."* What she actually meant was would I please let her have two different types of T-shirt which we were distributing as part of a cancer charity fund-raising event.

Cancer has overtaken heart disease as the major cause of death. This is partly due to the fact that, through lifestyle changes, many people have reduced their susceptibility to heart disease. Now it is time to apply lifestyle changes in order to reduce the incidence of some cancers, for which there is a strong correlation between how we live and the likelihood of developing the disease. Cancer researchers say that up to 50% of all the cancers we develop are avoidable.

A good starting point is to look at the chemical arsenal most of us keep in our houses. Deodorants, especially those supplied in aerosol form, are known to be harmful. We can choose to use soap and water more frequently and deodorants containing aluminium less often. In our cleaning cupboards, most of us have a huge array of cleaners clearly labelled with health warnings. Some are marketed for kitchen use while others specify that they are for bathrooms only. General purpose cleaner or good old-fashioned vinegar, which is a natural product, often do the job just as well.

Of even greater concern are the incredibly powerful chemicals used for "difficult" jobs such as oven cleaning. If the instructions indicate that protective clothing, eye cover or strong ventilation is needed for any product, including paint, we should be aware that it is potentially very harmful. In chemistry classes at school, we learned not to mix chemicals, unless we knew in advance what the reaction was going to be. This is a rule which on occasions, we break in our homes, such as when we pour both bleach and lavatory cleaner into the toilet, producing noxious chlorine gas.

The equivalent of a busload of people die every week as a result of malignant melanoma which are cancerous moles. If not removed quickly, these can allow cancer cells to travel into the lymph nodes and into major organs such as the liver and lungs with fatal consequences. It is paradoxical that in our determination to look supremely young and healthy, we cause rapid and irreversible degeneration of our skin. We do indeed need exposure to sunlight as this is the only way in which the body can produce vitamin D. Moreover, allowing our skin to produce small amounts of melatonin is beneficial. The problems arise when we overdo it: when we go on holiday and "binge" sunbathe and when we "make the most" of our brief summer and work all day in the garden with our shirt off.

Even if we do not develop cancer, all exposure to the sun will cause loss of elasticity in the skin, which is one of the indicators of age. Therefore the more we expose ourselves to direct sunlight, the older we will look. By contrast, there is a woman who loves living in warm climates. She likes to joke that she will only live in countries where frangipani and bougainvillea grow. Now in her early 50s, despite being fair skinned and having lived half her life in the tropics, she has incredibly youthful and beautiful skin. The reason for this is that she always applies a UV screening cream to her face and hands first thing in the morning, regardless of the country she is in or what the weather looks like outside.

A subject of even greater taboo than sex, for general conversation, is defecation. The efficiency of the flushing toilet, commercialised by the eponymous Thomas Crapper, and the hidden, subterranean sewage system that surreptitiously removes our waste, allows us to pretend that human defecation does not take place. This, despite the fact that we are all totally aware that every living animal takes in food and eliminates that which is unusable.

Evolution took a massive step forward when simple organisms no longer took in nutrients and expelled unwanted matter through the same opening. Rather, like an earthworm, an intestinal tract developed allowing the intake of material at one end and the expulsion of detritus at the other. More efficient and much more palatable, unless of course you come from the Oxbridge school of thought, which claims that a good time to vomit is after drinking champagne. That way you can enjoy it both on the way down and on the way up.

Cancers of the colon and rectum are relatively common and a leading cause of death. It is known, however, that certain diets contribute to, or help avoid these cancers. A diet high in red meat and animal fat is more likely to lead to colorectal cancer than one containing a high percentage of fibrous material such as that found in fruit and vegetables.

A young nurse was surprised when, shortly after marriage, her sick husband was shocked and embarrassed, not wanting her to examine his stools. Her attitude, like much of the medical profession throughout time, was that scatological examination provided valuable information about the health of the patient. At one boys school, a well-meaning biology master tried to approach the subject by telling his pupils that they should be producing stools which were light in colour and floated. This he said indicated a sufficient volume of fibrous material in the diet. In turn, this led to the question being asked around the school, "Do you produce sinkers or swimmers?"

A dietician phrased things somewhat differently. She said that the colon needs to be kept clean by the regular passage of unprocessed and fibrous material which sweeps all before it. If food material, especially meat is allowed to remain in the colon for too long, its degeneration will create the conditions in which cancer can occur. Her recommendation was an occasional "housecleaning." Specifically, she suggested taking two tablespoons of golden linseed, soaking them in water for a couple of hours and then drinking. The linseeds are full of omega oil which is good for us and the husk of the seed gives a cleansing bulk to the stool. She said that an ideal stool would be soft, uniform in shape and after passing would not require the use of toilet paper.

The charity organisation "Beating Bowel Cancer" encourages people to eat more fruit and vegetables saying that, "*There is clear and growing evidence for the protective effects of fruit and vegetables against chronic diseases.*" Eating at least five portions of fruit and vegetables a day, on average, could lead to estimated reductions of up to 20% in overall deaths from chronic diseases, such as coronary heart disease, stroke and some cancers. Experts regard increasing fruit and vegetable consumption as the second most important strategy for cancer prevention after reducing smoking.

Sexually Transmitted Diseases – The "sword of Damocles" which hangs over anyone enjoying sex with a new or unknown partner is the potential for contracting (or passing on) one of the many sexually transmitted diseases. These range from the uncomfortable but curable, to the highly painful, greatly debilitating and ultimately fatal. One actress who had suffered from a severe case of venereal disease joked that she "had had the clap like a standing ovation." For most sufferers of sexually transmitted diseases, they are not a laughing matter. Each and every one of us has the choice and opportunity to protect ourselves and our partners as much as possible by using condoms and practising safer sex.

As John Wilkes, MP, writing to the Earl of Sandwich said, "*Whether I die on the gallows or die of the pox depends on whether I embrace your politics or your mistress.*"

A recent survey of the sexually active found that one in ten men think that Chlamydia is the name of a flower. While their lack of horticultural knowledge is not significant, their lack of awareness about the most common sexually transmitted disease is. In women, there may be no obvious symptoms, or symptoms which do not appear to be related, such as cystitis or a change in vaginal discharge. In men, it may be more apparent because of a urethral discharge. With both men and women, the symptoms may disappear but they are still infectious and able to pass on the disease. Chlamydia has long been associated with infertility in women. Current research suggests that it is also a cause of infertility in men.

There is a long list of very unpleasant diseases which are transmitted through sexual contact. They include genital herpes, gonorrhoea, syphilis, HIV and genital warts. In a particularly unpleasant case of the latter, a nurse described a man's penis as looking like "corn on the cob." Everyone who is sexually active can make themselves aware of these diseases and the circumstances under which they are at greatest risk. It is obvious that the more sexually active we are, or our partner is, the greater the overall risk of passing on or contracting a venereal disease. In the late 19th century it is thought that the majority of London's numerous prostitutes had syphilis. They truly could have been "femmes fatales".

The only sure way to be fully protected is through abstinence. As this is neither practical nor desirable, it is appropriate to understand what is required to practise safe sex. Even here, we must recognise that there is no such thing as completely safe sex. There is only "safer sex" depending on the sexual acts performed and the level of protection. One policeman from Cardiff joked that for many teenage girls their only idea of protection was to use a bus shelter.

Basically speaking, the aim of safe sex should be to avoid the exchange of bodily fluids, especially blood and semen. Use of a latex condom, which is both fitted and removed with care, will provide the maximum protection for the minimum investment in effort and inconvenience. Each of us knows the type of lifestyle we lead and we can make suitable preparations well before we have a sexual encounter, especially if there is any likelihood that our judgment will be impaired by that sexual lubricant, alcohol.

Protect your hearing. There is a young man with an almost perfect physique. Broad shoulders, well-defined muscles, a slim waist and an enviable "sixpack." His body developed this way naturally as a result of his work as a driveway layer. This involves lifting and carrying endless amounts of stone slabs. This same young man has now lost his hearing in one ear and is partially deaf in the other. This is due to the fact that the masonry cutting machine he uses is very loud. With the bravado of youth, he thought it was unnecessary to wear ear protection.

This may sound like an extreme case and perhaps it is. Nevertheless many young people are constantly exposing themselves to sound levels which will, without doubt, seriously impair their hearing in later life. Personal music systems which are constantly played too loudly have been proven to cause early loss of hearing. The Royal National Institute for Deaf People recommends noise cancelling headphones, preferably "over-the-ears" type rather than using sheer volume in "ear bud" headphones to block out external noise.

The entertainment industry which includes cinemas, but more importantly nightclubs, is a major risk. In an attempt to take control of our senses with incredibly high decibel sound systems, they quite literally assault and damage our eardrums. It may not be "cool" but anyone such as bar staff and DJs who spend a lot of time in these places should consider wearing ear plugs.

Regardless of whether or not a particular illness can be prevented, we all have the choice of developing awareness about the causes and effects as well as the symptoms of disease. We should be aware that self examination for breast or testicular cancer can lead to early diagnosis and affect our own longevity. Over and over again, we see that diet, our weight and our level of exercise directly affect our health. It is up to us to take responsibility for our own bodies. Prevention in the form of sensible eating, controlling our weight and taking exercise are far better than expecting the medical profession to repair the damage that we ourselves have caused.

Anyone who has had a serious accident looks back with regret, wishing that they had not put themselves into that particular situation of risk. With poor diet, drinking, smoking, obesity, lack of exercise and sexually transmitted diseases we are at choice. We all have the option to overindulge, to abstain completely or to consciously plan our behaviour in order to maximise our enjoyment of life, while minimizing the chances of developing an avoidable or self-inflicted illness.

DRUGS: USE AND ABUSE

"Ecstasy, a drug so strong it makes white people think they can dance" – Lenny Henry.

First of all a confession. I use recreational drugs, the most obvious of which is alcohol. Mostly wine and beer, but the form in which I take it really does not matter. I also use coffee. Note the word "use" is relevant because I do use the caffeine in my morning pot of coffee to kick-start me into action. There was also a time when I took a lot of liver damaging "over the counter" decongestant tablets to alleviate the symptoms of sinusitis.

All commonplace, legal and boring I hear you say, especially as 80% of the world's population uses caffeine every day. This hardly puts me into the same league as some Americans who proudly wear a T-shirt proclaiming, *"I'd rather be snorting cocaine off a hooker's ass."* But they are drugs nevertheless, so let's start with the coffee.

Many years ago when I worked in the US for a large American corporation, there was a ritual which took place at 10.30 every morning. A trolley would arrive in our department with ample fresh coffee and a mountain of doughnuts. We all looked forward to our mid-morning break and inevitably some of us started to glance at our watches any time from 10 o'clock onwards. It was a social occasion during which we chatted about everyday interests such as sport and television. The company presumably felt that this was a useful way of bonding the team together.

It could however be looked at in a different way. Like Pavlovian dogs, we started to salivate before the appointed time, waiting to be given our little reward. There is no doubt that the combination of caffeine and sugar gave us an enormous boost, and when we returned to work we did so with high energy, albeit short lived. The problem is that caffeine and sugar do not really increase energy. Sugar is quickly absorbed and rapidly raises the level of blood sugar. The body counteracts this by releasing insulin and can have the effect of making us feel less energetic than before receiving the sugar boost.

Drugs

Almost everyone is aware of the dangers of illicit drugs. Incredible to most people is the fact that prescribed drugs control the lives of far more people than those which are illegally obtained. Worse still is the hidden, but enormously high, number of deaths caused by prescription and over-the-counter drugs. There are numerous examples of show business stars who have died from the abuse of legally prescribed drugs. They include Elvis Presley, Marilyn Monroe, Heath Ledger and Michael Jackson. The pressures and financial leverage found in show business, together with the publicity surrounding the addiction of a well-known person, make it seem as if this is a problem unique to the famous. Sadly, the rest of us mere mortals are affected just as badly, though not as obviously. Huge numbers of ordinary working people become addicted to antidepressants, strong painkillers and even some cough mixtures which contain opiate-like ingredients.

Smoking

Smoking is the leading preventable cause of death in the world and tobacco is the only legal consumer product that kills one third to one half of those who use it. On average, it shortens the lifespan of those who use it by 15 years.

Alcohol

Homer Simpson famously said, *"Alcohol is the cause of and solution to all of life's problems."* This simple equation affects all of us, whether we drink or not. We are all affected by the enormous impact alcohol has on society, ranging from antisocial behaviour to the costs imposed on police and medical services.

Drinking alcohol is widely associated with leisure time activities, socialising and generally having fun. If we are invited to dinner or to a party, we normally expect alcohol to be served. We all know that it reduces our inhibitions. Other people's jokes, and more importantly our own, are much funnier after a few drinks. Alcohol is the social lubricant which allows us to connect more easily with other people. Like all habits and addictions, we would not engage in drinking if there were no rewards and benefits.

The "enfant terrible" of the film world, the actor Robert Downey Jr., claims to have been given marijuana by his father at the age of eight. He readily admits to substantial drug taking in later life, which in turn stalled his career and landed him in prison on more than one occasion. Despite all this, he is quoted as saying, *"I was a sober, non-smoking vegetarian once, and was never so miserable in my whole life. There was nothing, nowhere to go."*

One friend told me that, when starting a new relationship, she was advised by her friends to get the new man drunk. That way she would quickly get to know his real character. Over 2,000 years ago, the Romans said more or less the same thing in their expression "In Vino Veritas" – in wine the truth.

Koren Zailckas who became an alcoholic after starting to drink at 14, wrote a revealing book entitled, "Smashed." She talks about the seduction of the liquor industry; the name Southern Comfort, which made her think of warm apple pie. She goes on to say that liquor industry advertising, which targets the young, only depicts happiness and good times. The implication being that you are an adult proving your individuality and doing "your own thing." The truth for her, however, was that she was shy, self-conscious and lonely. She drank because she was unhappy.

The liquor industry extols us, especially before Christmas, to use alcohol wisely. It preaches moderation while at the same time associating liquor with good times. It is like driving with one foot on the brake and the other on the accelerator. The undeniable fact is that alcohol reduces our inhibitions. Those inhibitions include the ability to be moderate.

Despite being a drinker myself, and counter to virtually every society throughout known history, I anticipate that attitudes towards drinking will change. Quite possibly within the next couple of generations, the pendulum of public opinion will swing from the idea that drinking is socially normal and acceptable to an abhorrence of it, matching today's attitude towards smoking. The enlightened belief will be that drinking is harmful to us as individuals and to society as a whole.

This timeframe may even be speeded up by the scientists at Imperial College London who are developing a synthetic and more focused alcohol replacement which gives users all the enjoyable, inhibition-lowering benefits of liquor, but none of the disadvantages. Better still, there is to be an antidote which provides the ability to switch the drug off, so users can sober up quickly and will even be able to drive home safely.

Marijuana

Marijuana is an euphoria-inducing drug which still confuses and causes endless debate. Middle-aged, middle-class parents who grew up in the 1960's and 70's and who are violently anti-drugs, look back fondly on their pot smoking student days. There is a feeling that marijuana is all right because it is not a "hard" drug. The specious argument is used that it is no more harmful than alcohol, which is socially acceptable and is legal

Others argue that marijuana is a hallucinogen just like acid and LSD. Like these drugs, it may cause irreversible psychotic damage. Moreover much of the "weed" currently on our streets today is in fact "skunk", which is far stronger and much more habit forming than basic marijuana. What is known is that cannabis does affect our neurotransmitters. It does affect short-term memory and can trigger irreversible personality disorders in some people.

If we are already in good health we can choose (illegally) to take the short term gain of euphoria from marijuana, cocaine or any other drug. We should not, however, do this without being realistic about the very high price we might have to pay such as long-term risks to our physical health, dependency and mental impairment.

Heroin

Heroin offers all of us the ultimate high and the ultimate degradation. A recent television programme about drug use showed a dirty and dishevelled woman in appalling physical condition injecting heroin into her heel. When asked why she did this, she said that heroin gave her an incredible sense of pleasure. It was like having an orgasm which could last for two or three hours. But she warned that the addiction and need for heroin is so urgent that she guaranteed it would dominate and destroy the life of anyone who ever used it. Nothing and no-one in their life would be more important than heroin. Everything, including family members, would be used, abused and violated in the constant search for the next hit.

People do not make a conscious decision to become addicted. All addiction is caused by choosing an inappropriate response to a deep seated need. Feelings of boredom, loneliness, inadequacy and powerlessness. Many of us find an overly simplistic and dangerous solution to our need. This need has itself sometimes been referred to as "the hole in the soul."

THE FOOD WE EAT

"Good food, good wine and good company enrich our lives beyond measure"- Stephen Fry

Getting enough to eat is our most basic instinct and our greatest driving force. In nature, animals spend most of their time searching for food. When, like grass, it is readily available they spend most of their time consuming it in order to take in sufficient nutrition. Eating is nature's top priority after avoiding immediate danger, and comes before everything else, including reproduction.

We humans vary in our access to food. We all know that there are vast swathes of the world in which getting enough to eat is a daily struggle. There are also millions of people who spend virtually all of their modest resources on food. It takes priority over education and medical care. How the rest of us think about food should always be put into the context of how fortunate we are to have choice in this matter.

There are numerous television shows devoted to cookery and our weekend newspapers have endless restaurant reviews. As critics extol the virtues of one dish or denounce another, they think only of the relative pleasures which food can provide and rarely mention nutritional values. This idea, juxtaposed with hunger in the developing world, does at first glance appear obscene. But, of course, there is absolutely nothing wrong with pleasure. Just because nature's primary reason for sex is reproduction does not mean we should not enjoy it. Just because we ingest food to gain nutrition does not mean that we should not enjoy the process.

Hunger pangs and oral pleasure have evolved to give us the strongest possible motivation to eat and enjoy eating. That leaves some human beings with a dilemma, unique in the animal kingdom. We are motivated by pleasure to eat and many of us have the economic resources to eat as much as we want.

Animals, ranging from dormice to bears, eat all they can when food is plentiful. Nature knows that they will need stocks of fat to fuel them through the long winter hibernation. Even though we might like to, we human beings do not hibernate through the winter. If we take advantage of our ability to eat more than we need, we will gain excess fat, which for us is a health risk not a survival advantage.

We can decide whether "a moment on the lips is worth a lifetime on the hips." Also worth considering is that we have to burn off 3,500 more calories than we consume to shed one pound of fat. Or we can remember the following rough equation. One large chocolate muffin could contain 450 calories. One hour of medium exercise on a rowing machine is required to burn 450 calories.

In an ideal world, we would consume only the number of calories that we need in order to offset the lifestyle we lead. Our food intake would release the right amount of energy when needed. Our diet would include foods which gave us all the vitamins and minerals needed by our bodies. It would also include sufficient fluid to keep us well hydrated and sufficient fibre to keep our intestinal tract healthy. If wonderful taste, texture and appearance could be added to such food, we would have the perfect formula. Sounds simple, doesn't it?

Most of us eat out of habit according to the social patterns of the culture in which we live. We have breakfast, lunch and dinner interspersed with cups of tea and perhaps a snack. We eat an inordinate amount of pre-prepared food ranging from breakfast cereals to convenience meals without really knowing whether the ingredients are good for us. Meals may fill our stomachs and satisfy our hunger but may not adequately nourish us. We are seduced by and sometimes addicted to salt, sugar and various forms of fat, all of which are far more limited in the natural diet of most animals.

What we can do is increase our awareness about food and then choose what to eat and in what quantity. Simply by reducing the amount of processed foods we eat, we can greatly improve our diet. Supermarkets have an enormous array of breakfast cereals, most of which are designed to appeal to children. They are over-refined and highly sugared. One cereal sold in the United States is said contain as much sugar in each serving as is found in a bar of chocolate. Sugar contains so much energy that in some sugar cane producing countries like Brazil and India it is fermented into alcohol and used as automotive fuel.

If we consume more sugar than we are able to burn off through exercise, our bodies will store that energy as fat. Advertisements will often claim nutritional benefits for a bowl of their cereal to which milk is added. What is not mentioned is that much of the nutritional advantage comes from the milk and not from the cereal itself. Even the so-called healthy option cereals vary enormously. A product may claim legitimately that it has no added sugar but if it contains large quantities of dried and crystallized fruit, it still contains a high level of sugar.

Whether or not we eat meat is an entirely personal decision. Vegetarians will cite the fact that we are so closely, genetically, related to most animals that eating them is little different to cannibalism. Non-vegetarians will note that throughout nature animals eat other animals (sometimes even from the same species), and that it is completely normal for us to do so. Yet others will say that domestic cattle are only bred for the purpose of being eaten and would therefore have no life at all without this sequence.

In this era of environmental concern, we must acknowledge the fact that many more people can be fed using vegetable protein than by using grass land and grain itself to raise animals for meat. We in the West should not abuse the power our wealth gives us and learn to reduce our animal protein consumption.

There is the old adage that we are what we eat. The quality of the food we eat is important, both for health and for pleasure. Large-scale modern farming routinely sprays crops, including vegetables and fruit, with pesticides. Battery-reared chickens as well as farmed salmon are fed diets laced with growth hormones and antibiotics, which we then ingest. Anyone who is lucky enough to have eaten a chicken which has scratched around in the farmyard or plucked an imperfect apple off an old tree from the bottom of someone's garden will be astounded by the wonderful natural taste.

Right up until the 1970s, the food we ate at home was fully prepared in the home. Vegetables were peeled and dishes such as casseroles were slowly cooked in the oven. This may have been a time-consuming process but it did mean that we retained and absorbed all the nutrients and natural goodness from our food. The proliferation of ready meals and the use of the microwave is a two-edged sword. On the one hand, we have the benefit of saving time, but the price we pay for this is both a loss of basic nutritional value and more importantly, the absorption of a wide range of additives and preservatives. When a large commercial organisation, such as a supermarket, prepares our food, we lose control over what goes into it.

Worse still is the fact that, in a perverse form of evolution, much of the current generation has never developed even the most rudimentary food preparation skills. So if we wish to eat wholesome nutritional food it is worthwhile learning the basics of cooking. Many people who do enjoy cooking see it as a pleasure and as a hobby, not as a chore. Most fortunate of all are those people who see cooking as an act of love. They see it as a privilege to prepare food and share it with their family and friends.

Even as recently as 40 years ago, chicken, and especially salmon, were considered to be luxury foods. Relative to income, they were expensive commodities. A century ago most of the food we ate was fresh, unprocessed and naturally produced. As time went by, it was considered a luxury to have white bread. Other foods became more and more refined, including "tooth rotting" white sugar, which we consumed in ever increasing quantities. The more we refine food, the less fibre it contains. The very fibre that is essential for the elimination of waste and keeping the intestinal tract clean.

Relative to our incomes, food has continued to become less and less expensive. Sadly, it has also become less and less nutritious and beneficial. Our supermarkets are crammed with "reformed meats," dairy substitutes and pre-prepared meals speciously advertised as being "healthy option." One choice we have is to eat less food but to invest in genuinely healthier, more natural, better quality food. We can eat slowly, savouring both the taste and texture, celebrating our food as nutrition and enjoying it as one of life's natural pleasures.

We can at the same time listen to Oprah Winfrey's mantra that we should eat to satisfy our nutritional needs rather than our emotional ones. Or we can remember Joan Collins' advice, *"The best exercise for loosing weight is to push away from the table."*

FITNESS AND EXERCISE

Unless we are an athlete, most of us do not give much thought to our fitness until an occasion arises when our body does not perform as we would like. We start to notice our health when we get out of breath more quickly than we would expect, or find that it is harder to bend down and lace up our shoes.

The majority of the young are blessed with natural fitness. They enjoy running around, riding a bicycle and climbing. In doing so, they develop their muscles and their motor skills. Many will continue to be involved in a variety of sports. For others, their time will be spent working hard to launch their careers and socialising with their friends, possibly in a pub. Then as time goes by the natural fitness and flexibility which youth gave them starts to disappear.

Many people drift through middle age vaguely aware "that they should be doing more exercise" but continue to do very little. Their bodies are still functioning at a reasonable level: that is, they can move around the house and workplace easily enough and still play the occasional round of golf. This apparent well-being has the potential to be quite dangerous. In the winter in Canada, doctors know that there will be an increase in heart attacks. This is because otherwise sedentary men go out and strenuously shovel snow or help a neighbour push his car off an icy patch.

We live in an ageist society. We dismiss the elderly precisely because they do move more slowly, lack physical strength and find it difficult to move in certain ways. Formerly upright people now stoop. Sadly, many of the elderly view themselves in the same way, feeling that it is inevitable that their bodies and minds will continue to deteriorate.

Just as we plan for the future in our jobs and private lives, so we should plan for our own physical future. I would assume that most people would want their bodies to perform well for them throughout their lives. That is we should retain as much mobility as possible. In order to do this, we need to have a strong heart and plaque-free arteries. Our lungs need to be exercised regularly in fresh air and our bodies need to be kept as supple as possible.

At one time I lived in a seaside village which was nestled in a valley between two hills. Every day, morning and evening, I saw an old lady walking her dog up one of the hills and along the cliff path at the top. Whether or not she was conscious of it, I do not know, but she had found the perfect recipe for staying fit. Twice a day she had wonderful exercise for her heart and lungs. She exercised most of her muscles and, in so doing, maintained a healthy bone mass. She had a sense of purpose in taking her dog out, and as she also chatted with other walkers she kept her mind active and felt involved in village life. For her, walking the dog was a pleasure, not an exercise chore. Perhaps that is the secret. We must find a lifestyle which we enjoy and which is also healthy and beneficial to us.

Being conscious of our physical health and taking firm steps to promote it is beneficial not only physically but also mentally. When we know that our body is healthy and working well, we are more likely to feel emotionally and psychologically upbeat. We can look towards the future with optimism.

Everyone says the same thing – that the hardest part about an exercise programme is getting started. We must get over the inertia and start taking regular exercise.

One of the big fears about going to a gym is that everyone else there will be super fit and will have a perfect body. The reality is quite different. In most gyms, there is a complete age range including those who are overweight, those who are underweight, those who are new to exercise and those who have already attained a level of fitness. The one common goal is that everyone wishes to improve their fitness in some way.

Getting fit and staying fit should not be seen as a daunting challenge. An awareness that we want to change and improve is the starting point. From then on, we simply have to adopt a lifestyle which is conducive to good health.

Any exercise programme should balance three key elements: aerobic exercise, such as that obtained from using a treadmill or cross-trainer: bone and muscle strengthening resistance exercises, such as using weights and: stretching exercises in order to maintain flexibility.

FINANCIAL FREEDOM

The British class structure reached its pinnacle in the Victorian and Edwardian eras. Simply stated, the upper-class had capital and financial resources which freed them from the requirement to be employed. Anyone who needed a job or needed to work for someone else was, in reality, if not by generally accepted definition, working-class.

The expression that "money cannot buy you happiness" is quite true, but a lack of money can cause considerable difficulty and distress. It has been said that marriage can survive adultery, but not debt. Insufficient financial resources are a major worry for many individuals and families. Everyone has basic financial needs which include the buying of food, the provision of somewhere to live, the payment of utilities and quite probably the need to pay for some type of transportation. Our first financial goal, therefore, is to have sufficient resources to meet our basic needs.

In most Western societies, it is usually possible to meet our basic needs, although this does not provide a particularly comfortable lifestyle. For those who are genuinely unable to work, there is basic provision of public assistance. In the majority of areas, there are jobs available. Admittedly, many of these jobs will pay the minimum wage and, if these are in high rent areas, there is undoubtedly a struggle to make ends meet. We must all sympathise with those who are trapped in such a financial squeeze. Oscar Wilde said, "*Teaching the poor to be thrifty is like telling the starving to eat less.*"

Sales of lottery tickets are far higher in poor countries and poor communities than they are in the more affluent. Purchasing a single lottery ticket is a fairly inexpensive way of giving some credence to our daydreams of wealth. How optimistic or desperate we human beings must be to do this. The fact is that when we purchase a lottery ticket the odds against winning are far greater than the chances that we will develop a terrible disease or die in some appalling accident. Yet we pin our hopes on being lucky in the financial lottery and avoiding the health one.

Purchasing a large number of lottery tickets or any other form of gambling is statistically a waste of money. For those who become too involved in gambling, there is a saying, "*You bet, far more debt.*"

All of us, but especially the less well-off, constantly have to decide on two important issues. First, we must ensure that whatever resources we have are used for the payment of essential expenses. We must make sure the rent is paid before we decide to spend an evening in the pub. We must ensure that the utility bills are paid before we decide on the luxury of a take-out meal.

Secondly, the other decision we have to make relates to our use of credit. Just as cigarette packages now carry very strong health warnings, so too should credit cards. For a start, the name should be changed to "debt cards." When we spend using a "credit" card, we create a debt for which we are responsible. Not only do we have to repay the debt but we then carry the additional burden of paying interest. The so called "credit limit" is a limit set by self-serving money lenders. It is not a target to be achieved by the fiscally irresponsible. For anyone struggling financially, the worst thing they can possibly do is incur additional and unnecessary costs such as the paying of interest. Being poor is bad enough, but being poor and having increasing debt is far worse.

Throughout history, there has been a universal suspicion and abhorrence of money lenders. Except in cases of usury or extortion, perhaps this is somewhat unfair given that in the transaction of lending money, unpaid creditors are the injured party, not the debtors. In the past, money lenders were at least known and recognised within their community. Now they are large faceless organisations working behind the prestigious façades of major banks. For better or worse, our communication with modern-day money-lenders is controlled through endless telephone menu choices which eventually lead to an anonymous Call Centre.

Credit cards do have advantages. They remove the necessity to carry large sums of cash and offer a convenient method of payment. But then so do debit cards. If credit cards are used for their convenience and paid off in full at the end of each month, they are worth having. If they lead the user into debt and the payment of interest, they are best avoided.

As recently as the 1970s, many people were still paid in cash. They then used the cash for all of their transactions ranging from the purchase of food to the payment of rent. Using cash rather than credit gives a far more realistic sense of money. We either have it, or we do not. If we do not have cash in our pocket, we are less likely to order another round of drinks which can only be paid for by going into debt. There were always people willing to lend money and take advantage of the poor. But the majority of people, through lack of "credit," managed to avoid the debilitating effects of debt. They lived in a culture of thrift, a concept to which we should return.

Today there is a frequently found "worst case" scenario in which people add to their debt in order to pay the required interest. Credit card companies allow us to pay off an extremely small percentage of the debt we incur. It is to their advantage to keep us in as much debt as possible, so long as we continue to pay the high rates of interest. So the debt, and the problems related to debt, compound and multiply like an aggressive form of financial cancer.

The seriously indebted run the risk of being seduced by slick advertising into the apparent comfort of what is euphemistically called "debt consolidation." They should beware, however, of

"Clause 78." This legally binds the borrower to the obligation of paying all anticipated interest and charges, even if at some time in the future the original debt is paid off. In other words, once someone who was already in debt falls for the bait of consolidation, they may be committing themselves to paying interest charges which could conceivably no longer apply.

As Charles Dickens said in David Copperfield, "*Annual income twenty pounds, annual expenditure nineteen pounds, nineteen shillings and six pence. Result happiness. Annual income twenty pounds, annual expenditure twenty pounds and six pence. Result misery.*"

In modern parlance, the same idea is understood by the statement, "*When we can no longer service our debt, we are in serious trouble.*"

When we are at a stage when we can pay for all of our basic requirements, we have reached an important financial position. We are no longer drowning, but are now able to keep our heads out of water. From now on, with careful management, things can get better. Now is the time to think about our financial goals and set a strategy for achieving them.

However young we, are it is worth looking into the future. We must optimistically assume that we will live into our 80s or 90s. Therefore financial planning must be part of long-term planning. At what age do we think we would like to stop working? When we reach that stage and have no employment income, how do we expect to survive? We will still have to live somewhere, buy food and use some form of transportation.

If we have rented accommodation throughout our lives, it will be necessary to continue to pay rent until we die. If that is the case, we must make sufficient provision not only to be able to pay the rent after we retire, but also to be able to cope with inflationary costs. In some countries, such as Germany, a far higher percentage of people rent accommodation throughout their working lives. Sometimes they will buy their first house at the time of retirement. Others will just continue to rent.

Some people in the United Kingdom think that they have found a solution by purchasing lower-priced property in other lower-cost parts of Europe. This may work immediately after retirement when people are still healthy and mobile. From retirement onwards, however, we know that our health will decline and it therefore seems sensible to plan for this eventuality – to remain close to our families, to be in a country where we can speak the language and to ensure that we receive adequate medical care.

My own feeling is that we should all try to own a mortgage-free property, however modest, by the time we retire. We then need to have sufficient money to pay taxes and live in whatever style we aspire to. In order to own a property, we must start with the apparently simple process of buying one. But, as we all know, it is not quite that simple. We must raise the down payment on a property, qualify for a mortgage and have the ongoing means to meet the mortgage payments.

I do not for one minute wish to imply that this is easy. The ratio of property prices to incomes is higher now than at any time before. Added to this, many young people wishing to purchase their first home may still be paying off debts from their higher education. Notice again the terrible impediment of debt. It drags like a sea anchor preventing any real forward movement. So if there is anyone reading this who is still incurring debts from education, they should ask themselves if there is any way in which they can eliminate or at least minimise the growth of their debts.

Does their study schedule allow enough time to work at a part-time job? In the United States, where there have always been university fees, it is considered absolutely standard for people to "work their way" through college. In North America, there are also many young people who continue to live at home while attending the closest university or college. This may not be as much fun as living the life of total freedom away from parental constraints, but it is a logical way to minimise the accumulation of debt.

There used to be a joke at Cambridge which said, *"Most students went there to study, to play sports and to chase members of the opposite sex ... and most of them managed to do two out of three."* There is no doubt that many courses such as medicine, engineering and architecture do require huge effort and leave little time for earning money. Most Arts courses are substantially less demanding, especially in the first year. Many students are so bored and lethargic as a result of their undemanding study schedule that they sink into what they consider to be normal student life, sleeping in late and drinking too much beer. How much better if they got a part-time job to offset both the lethargy and the growing level of debt.

Another option would be to work full-time or part-time and to study with an educational institution which is supportive of this type of work/study arrangement. Birkbeck College in London, the Open University or any other college at which courses and outside employment can be dovetailed together. But it is much harder work, requiring far greater self-discipline and less fun than the normal format of higher education. This choice, like all choices, is open to the individual. They can decide whether to take the easy path or the hard path. To work hard and avoid debt or to indulge in a hedonistic lifestyle, the result of which is often the incurring of debt, while working for a degree which may not be of any particular value in the workplace.

In the lavatory of the engineering faculty at a top university, there was some graffiti written just above the toilet roll which read, *"Arts degrees – take one."*

Students, and the parents of students, should ask why they are pursuing higher education. Is it to gain specific training in order to enter one of the professions? Is it because they have a keen interest in learning about a particular discipline? Is it because of the understandable feeling that in order to get that first job it is necessary to have a degree? Or is it now merely considered to be a rite of passage between leaving school and accepting the responsibilities of adulthood? Answering this question honestly should help substantially in choosing the most appropriate path towards higher education and deciding how much or how little debt to incur in the process.

The major cause of debt is that which results from overspending. If this statement sounds moronically obvious and simple, we have to ask why so many people do it. Another source of debt occurs when we fail to make provision for all of the taxes for which we are liable. Unless people have their income tax deducted by their employer, they will also become indebted to the government. It is a sobering thought that Inland Revenue is responsible for triggering more bankruptcies than all the major banks and lending institutions put together.

When we are in debt, we must plan ways in which to pay off or eliminate the debt. We should always start by paying off the most expensive debts. Usually this will be credit card debt which is generally in the range of 17.9%, but some loans such as store cards can be as high as 29% per year. It is worth remembering that mortgages frequently provide the lowest cost of borrowing money. As we pay tax on any interest we earn, it makes sense to use a bank account which combines and offsets savings and mortgage payments. These schemes work by offsetting an account holder's savings against their debts. This includes mortgage as well as personal indebtedness, such as outstanding credit card balance.

This is obvious when we hear the old joke that bankers work on the 6-8-2 formula. They pay their depositors 6%, charge borrowers 8% and they are on the golf course by 2 o'clock.

There are occasions when becoming indebted does make sense or is the only way to move forwards. The two most obvious examples of this are the purchase of property, which will inevitably require a mortgage, and the running of a business, which will almost always require a commercial line of credit.

The key to basic financial planning is to defer gratification until as late as possible. That is, we do not buy expensive, and possibly unnecessary, consumer items including things like exotic holidays until we are sufficiently financially secure to do so. Not a popular concept among the generation which grew up with affluence and consider it normal to have whatever they want, whenever they want it.

The reality for most people is that they cannot have it both ways. They cannot expend their income on maintaining a hectic social life and still save for a down payment or make contributions to a pension plan. Alison Steed wrote, "*If you think pensions are boring, how exciting do you think poverty in old age is going to be?*"

In one of his most popular songs, Freddie Mercury of Queen, screams out, "*I want it all ... I want it all and I want it NOW!*" In another song, he sings: "*Don't stop me now ... I'm having fun!*"

Great sentiments to express during the buzz of rock concert or in a club, but poor advice for the real world of fiscal planning.

Planning for and achieving financial freedom is just another choice. We can follow our own desires and submit to the peer pressure requirement of "having it now" or we can make provision for the future. Better still, if we can find a balance between profligacy and penury.

Change is occurring in our world at an unprecedented rate. The global financial powerhouses of the United States and Europe are in decline. We are used to an era in which the financial dominance and military strength of United States has, through their foreign policy, controlled and dictated what happened in much of the rest of the world. This is changing rapidly. All of us in the West feel rather smug at the moment. Our incomes allow us to purchase vast amounts of consumer goods which are relatively very cheap. These products are cheap because labour rates in countries like China are currently so very much lower than they are in the West.

It is not just products which are produced less expensively. Services, including high-tech jobs and research and development, as well as computer software programming are increasingly being undertaken by the huge number of well-educated graduates in countries like India. Again, it is because the salaries being paid to these people are substantially lower than those demanded in Silicon Valley or Cambridge.

Then there is oil. There is no denying the fact that we all consume energy, not just in our homes and transportation but in any type of commercial or manufacturing venture. Oil production in the United States and Europe is declining rapidly and has already reached a level where we in the West are net importers. The Middle East and Russia still have vast amounts of oil and natural gas. The fact that we need oil and they have it gives them substantial leverage over us.

In summary, we are facing an enormous shift in the balance of power. The United States and Europe are filled with people, who by global standards, are overpaid. So the jobs will move to other parts of the world, especially to China and India. Political control will be exerted by countries that hold key resources such as oil. The military and economic potential of China is enormous. They have a vast army and are increasingly investing in sophisticated military hardware. Countries and organisations hostile to the West are constantly trying to acquire nuclear weapons. Sooner or later, one of these will have the ability to engage in nuclear terrorism and even in a full scale nuclear war.

This is not scaremongering. This is an acceptance of the facts that are widely known and voiced on a regular basis. The reason for discussing it now is to highlight the fact that not only must we plan for the future but we must plan for a future that in all likelihood will be very different to the present.

MONEY

When a great barrister won an important case, his female
client rushed up to him and enthusiastically enquired as to how
she could ever repay him. *"Madam,"* he said, *"since the
Mesopotamians first invented money 5,000 years ago, there has
been no better way."*

When I was growing up, the expression used to describe
anyone of vast wealth was that they were a millionaire. Now as
the result of inflation, having a net worth of one million dollars or
even one million pounds is not uncommon. Today the measure of
substantial wealth is to be a billionaire.

The Roman historian Livy (Titus Livius) told us that in
ancient Rome wealth was calculated by how many asses someone
could notionally buy. That is, if they sold or traded all of their
belongings and acquired asses, how many could they buy? The
very rich could buy in excess of 100,000. But it has also been
estimated that for a Roman to live the same quality of life that we
all enjoy today, he would have needed at least 5,000 slaves;
musicians and performers to entertain him in the same way that
our iPods and television sets do, cooks to provide instant meals
just like our supermarkets and microwaves, and a host of servants
just to provide hot water, keep our houses warm and replace the
function of our flushing lavatories.

Rarity is the primary determining factor of value. Gold,
because of its rarity and its un-tarnishing beauty, has always been
the one true standard of value. Its purity can be tested by applying
nitric acid which dissolves all base metals but will not affect gold
– hence the expression "the acid test." The ancient Egyptians who

made Tutankhamun's death mask, thought of gold as the "flesh of the gods," radiantly beautiful and eternally incorruptible.

When we barter one item for another, there is no confusion. If we are trading an axe head for a sack of grain, we can examine the item we are acquiring and adjust our bid accordingly. As soon as we use some kind of currency, there is a large element of trust which convinces both parties that the currency is of reliable ongoing value.

During the 18th century, the London-based Hudson's Bay Company wanted to buy beaver pelts, used in the making of felt for top hats, from the North American Indians. When they found that the most popular form of payment for these pelts were woollen blankets, they started to manufacture different thicknesses of blanket. Each blanket was marked with a number of stripes depending on its size and weight. Each stripe represented a value of one beaver pelt. So through trust in the Hudson Bay Company's consistency, these blankets became a recognised form of currency.

Roman soldiers were sometimes partially paid in salt. It was an essential commodity of that time because of its much needed qualities as a food preservative. Having recognizable value, it was an acceptable form of payment from which we get the word salary. It also gave rise to the expression, "being worth his salt."

Much of the world from the United States to places like Hong Kong has units of currency which they call the dollar. This name came from silver mined in the town of Joachimsthal in the present-day Czech Republic. Silver coins minted in this town became known as "thalers." In due course, a range of silver coins which included the Spanish peso were all colloquially known as thalers. Due to a shortage of British currency in the British American colonies, various thalers were used. At the time of Independence, the United States chose the anglicised name of the thaler and so the dollar became their new unit of currency.

It is worth remembering that money is only an intermediary. Having a large bank balance or a stack of banknotes under the bed is useless beyond that amount which is needed to give us real or psychological assurance of our future security. The real value of money lies in the freedom it gives us from the impositions of other people. The power which money gives us is the power to live our lives in the way that we wish to live them.

In the last chapter about financial freedom, it was suggested that we should defer gratification if we are to accumulate assets. That advice is right and proper for the young, and probably for the middle-aged. Perversely, it is a characteristic of people who were financially cautious early on in life that they continue to live frugally and end up being too wealthy at the time of their death. The implication of this in any country that levies inheritance tax is that a portion of the accumulated wealth will be lost. In Britain, the Treasury is often the largest single beneficiary of poorly-planned wills.

The logical thing, as we approach or pass retirement age, would be to give away any assets we do not need. To give with warm hands before we die. The problem is that we do not know how much longer we will live and whether or not we will require additional funds for contingencies such as nursing care. Moreover, most of us want to retain the warm fuzzy feeling of wealth.

People who have a good relationship with their offspring often wish to pass on assets. That does not however mean that everything which parents have accumulated should automatically be devoted to that purpose. One sincere financial adviser suggested to his clients that before they pass on a substantial percentage of their wealth to their offspring, they should remember what happened to King Lear. An updated version of this play might bring in the added complication of children who subsequently divorce.

For parents who have worked hard to accumulate funds, this may be a time when they should reward themselves for their own discipline. This is a time to drive a more comfortable car and take better holidays. If in the past they have always stayed in three star hotels, this may be the time to upgrade by a star or two. One elderly couple who had spent a lifetime building up their business recently upgraded their flight plans. They rightly observed that if they did not travel in business class now, their children would do so later.

For us as individuals, unused money, like unused power or influence, might as well not exist. It is meaningless.

DO YOU HATE PAYING TAX?

The business writer Ian Cowie says that people's enthusiasm for various taxes rises and falls in inverse relation to the amount they expect to pay. And Will Rogers said that filling out income tax forms has made more liars out of the American people than golf.

Surely we all hate paying taxes. Whether money is coming to us in the form of income or going out in the form of expenditure, we will almost certainly lose some of it in tax. None of us will pay taxes voluntarily. It seems that what is legitimately and rightly ours is being removed by the overbearing force of the state. Why do our governments tax us?

Shortly after the break-up of the Soviet Union, a business trip took me to Russia. One dark evening we were driving in a suburb of St Petersburg. Fortunately, there was very little traffic because the slow moving car in front of us stopped abruptly for no apparent reason. No brake lights, no slowing down, just a sudden and complete stop. We could see that the car was at a peculiar angle. Had a wheel come off? No, what had happened was that an extremely large pothole had literally swallowed the right-hand front wheel of the car.

At that time in Russia, there was so much confusion and with such little effective organisation that virtually no tax was being collected either federally or by the municipalities. There was neither the money nor the infrastructure to repair the roads. Later that evening I walked down one of the main roads and was surprised to see many elderly people standing passively in the freezing cold, their backs to the wall, as pedestrians passed by. I remember noticing how pink their cheeks were. They were holding out various items of food such as a small loaf of bread or perhaps a few potatoes. They waited in the freezing cold hoping someone would finally buy these modest items.

I had certainly seen extreme poverty in developing countries. But these were people living in a country which had for many years been ahead of the United States in the space race. Even more sobering was that these people were Caucasians, just like me.

On another business visit to Russia, this time in midsummer, I went to the city of Ekaterinburg. I noticed many large buildings, rectangular, utilitarian and without any attempt at architectural style or embellishment. In fact, quite the reverse. They had been painted a uniformly depressing khaki colour. These were the factories which had produced tanks and other armaments. As in the rest of the former Soviet Union, these were state-run factories employing thousands of people. When the arms race was over, or at least in abeyance for Russia at that time, some of these factories theoretically changed to manufacturing items such as farm machinery and tractors.

In reality, there was very little production. The outside world did not want second-rate products and domestically there was no money to purchase them. The joke at this time was that the employees pretended to work and that the government pretended to pay them.

In its simplest form, the basic law of economics says that through labour or by offering a service we add value to raw materials. These are then sold, or bartered, at which time a profit is made. The more we add value to a product, the more gain we produce. That in turn gives us the ability to purchase other products and services. In so doing, we add to the overall economy, and if there is a healthy economy it is possible to levy and collect taxes.

There is a popular left wing misconception that large corporations are a blight on society. Tabloid newspapers enjoy printing banner headlines exclaiming what large profits are made by some of these companies. What must be remembered is that these profits are based on massive investment. Individually, if we have savings or investments we expect to make a return on those funds. As the level of our own individual investments are relatively low, so too are the returns. The ratio of return on investment may not, however, be substantially different.

Moreover, anyone who objects to globalization and the supposed avarice of big business should recognise the enormous contribution these organisations make to society. Large corporations not only pay corporation tax but are major employers which support hundreds or even thousands of families who also pay tax and continue the circulation of money. It is worth remembering that government itself does not manufacture anything and does not make any money. The ability of government to operate its own structure and fund social services is entirely dependent on taxes obtained from private sector initiative.

In a democratic society, we elect the government whose policies are most appealing to us. Those policies include expenditure on all of the major services and facilities we have come to expect in developed countries. Medical care, education, policing, support for those in need, defence and the transportation system. In short, we need a capitalist society which produces income from which taxes can be levied, which in turn provide the funds to create the type of society in which we wish to live.

If we think about it, most of us understand why we need to pay taxes. Just as we have a responsibility to pay our share of taxes, governments should also learn to operate fairly. The levying of windfall taxes is debatable but retroactively changing the laws relating to tax collection is outrageous. It has the potential to be costly for the taxpayer and undermine sensible planning.

The greatest problem in many poor African countries is their inability, or governmental unwillingness, to adopt systems which will allow the cycle of poverty to be broken. So endemic is bribery and corruption that these forms of monetary transfer take the place of normal taxation. This in turn means that the powerful can draw off vast sums of money without providing support to the poor, who in turn find it impossible to do little more than survive.

The word classical comes from the Latin "classicus," meaning "of the highest rank" In ancient Rome, it also meant "taxpayer" because only those of the highest rank paid taxes. In my early 20s, shortly after I started to work for a large corporation, I remember hearing a senior executive complaining about how much tax he had to pay. At that time I had no money in the bank and was struggling on a very low income. I can remember thinking to myself that I wished I had his problem. How nice to be in a position where I had to pay a lot of tax.

Since that time, I have paid a lot of tax. Do I like paying tax? No. Would I pay tax voluntarily? Honestly no! Do I understand the need and desirability to pay tax? Yes. Am I pleased that I am in a position where I have to pay tax? Yes.

The same philosophy can be applied to a lot of other situations. When my house needs to be repaired, I can either complain about the cost or rejoice in the fact that I have a house in which to live. When my car needs a new set of tyres, I can worry about the hassle and the cost, or remember how lucky I am to have a car. When there are expenses arising from my children's education, I have the choice of being frustrated and annoyed, or remembering that my family is the most important and worthwhile part of my life.

It is always worth remembering that many people in our own country and around the world would like to be in some of the situations and faced with some of the issues we consider to be problematic.

When we have taken care of our basic needs, how we interact with other people and the world around us is critical to our enjoyment of life. So in the next level we shall look at our loving and sexual relationships and our compatibility with the world around us.

LEVEL 3 - BELONGING AND LOVE

Relating to Other People and the World Around Us

RELATIVITY

Most people will have heard of Einstein's theory of relativity and, like me, do not fully comprehend it.

The basic concept of relativity is, however, understandable. Sir Isaac Newton originally developed a much simpler and more comprehensible idea. If, for example, a ball was thrown at 5 feet per second, both the thrower and a bystander would see the ball moving at this speed. However, if the thrower was standing on an object, such as a flat-bed truck, which was travelling at 10 feet per second, the thrower would see the ball moving at 5 feet per second while the bystander would see the ball moving at 15 feet per second. So the question becomes, is the ball travelling at 5 fps or 15 fps. The answer is that it is travelling at both speeds and that its speed is relative to the viewer.

Ah, not so, you may say, it is of course travelling at 15 fps. It is only an illusion or rather a delusion on the part of the person who is moving to think that the ball is only travelling at 5 fps.

We are all on a planet which is rotating at a speed of 1,670 km per hour and is also orbiting the sun at a speed of 107,300 km per hour. So, even while we are lying in bed, we are travelling at speed of 900 km per second. If we therefore ask ourselves the question, are we lying stationary in bed or are we travelling at 900 kilometres per second, the answer is that we are doing both, relative to the observer's position,

In our day-to-day lives we travel at varying earth-based speeds. Walking at about 3 miles an hour, driving in town at about 30 miles an hour and on the motorway in the region of 70 miles per hour. We still find it amazing when we travel in aircraft at over 500 mph. (Incidentally an observer, in space, watching an aircraft flying across the Atlantic Ocean could be forgiven for thinking that the plane was stationary and that the world was rotating underneath it.) Relative to the planetary speeds already discussed, we are barely moving. Man really only starts to move fast when, in the space shuttle, he breaks free of atmospheric friction and gravity to orbit the earth at speeds of 16,920 mph.

We are rather smug in our sense of abundant knowledge. Those things which we cannot explain are easily set aside as being mysteries. Those things which we cannot explain but which please us are elevated to the status of miracles. One of the most beautiful and atmospheric places I have ever visited is St. Catherine's monastery in the Sinai peninsular. It was built on the site of the burning bush. According to the Bible, this was a bush in the desert which burnt continually without ever consuming itself.

The first thing to understand is that the people who witnessed this, and who had in the past seen bushes flare up and burn in the desert, really did see a fire which burned endlessly. Their understanding was that this was a bush which was burning and it was therefore a miraculous sign from God. A more prosaic analysis of this real event came from an experienced oilfield geologist. He was used to working in parts of the world where pockets of subterranean gas occasionally leaked out through fissures in the rock. Once ignited by the sun, these could produce a flame which would go on burning until the conditions of the gas supply changed.

The truth for us is what we believe. Other people may believe something different, in which case their truth is different to ours. Real truth is therefore relative to the empirical accuracy of the knowledge on which we base our beliefs.

It is easy for us to laugh at our ancestors who thought that the world was flat. Relative to the size of the human body, what we can see around us looks like a flat plate interrupted with a few hills and mountains. It is only when we climb to the top of one of those mountains or look out to sea that we notice the formerly inexplicable curvature of the earth.

Our planet is enveloped in a breathable atmosphere comprising 78% nitrogen and 21% oxygen (plus a little argon and carbon). Standing on earth, we assume that this cocoon is endless in depth and indefinitely enduring. The best way to understand that it is not true comes from the amazing story of US Air force Captain, Joseph Kittinger. In 1960, Kittinger wanted to reach the edge of space. Wearing the most primitive type of pressure suit, he ascended in a gondola raised by a helium filled balloon. At 102,800 feet (just under 20 miles), he knew he had gone as high as he could. He bailed out of the gondola into the total darkness and went into freefall towards earth.

What surprised him was the complete silence. Despite reaching speeds in excess of 700 miles per hour, there was no rushing of wind. No flapping of his clothing. Complete silence. Nothing but the balloon rapidly disappearing above him and the earth rapidly increasing in size as he hurtled towards it. Not until he re-entered the earth's atmosphere did he become aware of the sensations that any normal parachutist experiences.

Unprotected by a space capsule, or even a plane when flying above 10,000 feet, this is the most frightening realisation that the atmosphere, our life sustaining atmosphere, is so thinly spread around our world. Seventy five percent of the earth's atmosphere is found within a mere six or seven miles above the earth's surface. The breathable atmosphere only extends to a height equivalent of twenty Empire State buildings stacked on top of each other. That is why climbers need oxygen while still actually on earth. In relative terms, our atmosphere is little more than a mist. In relative terms, it could be as ephemeral as a mist.

When we look at other people we immediately categorise them by age. They are young or old depending on our own age. At the age of nine, we think of someone who is twelve, as being old. In middle age, we do not notice a meaningful age gap of less than 10 years. In our later years, we become accustomed to the majority of people being younger than we are. What we should really celebrate is that our lives are all overlapping in this wafer thin slice of cosmic time.

It is now hugely fashionable to trace our family tree. I like many other people would like to know who my direct ancestors were. Most of us secretly hope that we are descended from powerful and influential ancestors, that some of their unique gifts have been passed down to us and are still pulsing through our veins. What we should remember is that all human beings are related. We may form different branches of the tree which are clearly identifiable through DNA testing, but we are one species, one family and come from the same origin.

Most of us rightly have a sense of awe about objects from the past. Whenever I am in an old building such as a 12th century tithe barn or 900-year-old church, I like to place my hand on one of the stone blocks. I then think back to the men who cut and laid this piece of stone. I feel a tentative connection with a different age and with people whose lives were very different to mine. In museums, we wonder at artefacts made by our fellow man around the world and throughout the millennia. The relevant connection is always with other human beings. Our ancestors.

The result of geological circumstances sometimes leaves us awestruck, such as those at the Gwent levels where we can still see the actual footprints left by a child in the mud 7,000 years ago. Or when archaeologists found the intact and well preserved burial of a man in the Pavaland cave, put there 30,000 years ago. Our personal measurement of time and its relevance is usually related to human lives.

In relative terms, man has only just appeared on this planet. Our earth was formed 4.54 billion years ago and the universe is thought to have come into existence 12-15 billion years ago. Our earth, like all other planets, will at some time in the future cease to exist. The long timescale for the collapse of our planet is so incomprehensible in terms relative to the human life span as to become a non issue. Moreover, there is every likelihood that mankind will follow the other 99.9 per cent of all species that ever existed on earth and die out for some reason, possibly through self destruction, prior to this.

Our earth is just one planet in our galaxy, the Milky Way. Galaxies consist of vast numbers of stars and planets. Let me repeat the expression "vast numbers" because we are talking about huge numbers – in the order of hundreds of billions. When we take into account the astronomers' calculation that there are in excess of 125 billion galaxies, each containing in excess of 100 billion stars and planets, most of us just cannot comprehend the vastness of the universe. One astronomer tried to make this more comprehensible by saying that there are more planets and stars in the universe than there are grains of sand on every beach on earth.

We can more readily understand the speed of light when we think about an experiment which is carried out on a daily basis. A laser beam is directed at the moon and then reflected back to earth from a mirror. The light takes approximately 2.5 seconds for the round trip, a distance of about 478,000 miles. A light year, the distance travelled by light through space in a year, is not in fact a measurement of time but rather one of distance. It takes light one year to travel 5.9 billion miles (5.9 million, million miles.) It would take 100,000 light years to cross our own relatively small galaxy.

Measuring the size of the universe is difficult and imprecise partly because we can only measure what we can see or know to exist. It is a sobering thought to remember that the very first primitive telescope was invented by Galileo a mere 400 years ago, in 1609. One estimate proposes that the universe is 156 billion light years across. We live on a little rock, significant only to us, within a truly vast place.

For us on earth, time is a constant, it is linear and as reliable as the other three dimensions, but science has shown that gravitational waves cause time to warp, bend and distort in space. So in space, time moves at differing speeds.

We are gradually adding to our minute knowledge about the universe.

As technology continues to advance, there is every likelihood that the ideas presented in science fiction, which we consider to be preposterous, will become reality. Interstellar, if not intergalactic travel, within the next few generations. After all, television, the home computer and mobile phone were considered to be science fiction just a few decades ago. A mere hundred years ago no one could have believed they would ever see those amazing machines called helicopters or believed it possible that a mass of metal the size of a Boeing 747 would ever fly, let alone carry hundreds of people around the world so quickly. Like flying, things that we dreamed of in the past have become reality. So, too, will things that we dream of today become reality in the future.

More prosaically, this morning I prepared my favourite breakfast – porridge. I took porridge oats from the cupboard, added soya milk and slowly cooked this on my hob. To make it really interesting, I threw in some sunflower seeds and some dried cranberries. All ready in 10 minutes.

But that is only the convenient tip of the iceberg. Farmers in different parts of the world had to grow the oats, the soya beans, the sunflowers and the cranberries. Arrangements had to be made to roll the oats, extract the sunflower seeds, prepare the cranberries and transport them, conveniently packaged, to a supermarket near me. When I turned the knob on my cooker, gas flowed out on demand. Gas which had been formed millions of years ago, deep below what is now the North Sea, between Scotland and Norway. For my convenience, and for corporate profit, men had risked their lives building offshore platforms, drilling deep into the seabed and then using huge turbines to pump the gas through a vast pipeline network to my house.

A hundred years ago more people worked on the land than in the towns. Many people grew much of their own food and made many of their own clothes. Today in the West, the majority of people will never have picked an apple off a tree and would struggle with even the most basic needlework.

A hundred years ago, few people were educated beyond the

basic level of reading and writing. The skills that were needed were learnt on the land or in apprenticeships. Today, despite our endless complaining, we do have an effective and comprehensive educational system. With ability and determination, everyone can learn as much as they want about almost any subject. Radio, television, the Internet, and of course traditional libraries offer us a cornucopia of knowledge. Relative to our forbears, we can choose to be interested in and knowledgeable about almost anything.

Relative to our forebears, we lead comfortable lives, smug in our apparently huge knowledge and sophistication. A mere hundred years ago, horses were still the primary form of transportation. The technology growth curve is more like an ice hockey stick, constantly rising at an exponential angle. The simplicity of life has changed irreversibly. Globalisation means that even if we wish to, we can no longer live in regional or even national isolation.

The global population in 1650 was 500 million and the growth rate was a mere three-tenths of one per cent, with life expectancy averaging about 30 years. This combination of factors would require a period of 400 years for the population to double. Yet by 1950 the population had grown to 2,500 million with a life expectancy of 53 years. Now we have a global population of in excess of 6,600 million and the forecast is that it will reach over 9,000 million by the year 2050. In other words, the 400 year period from 1650 to 2050 should theoretically have seen the global population double from half a billion to one billion. What we will actually see is a growth from half a billion to 9 billion.

The one thing that will have remained constant throughout the 400 years is the amount of dry land in the world. There were 14,000 million hectares in 1650 and there will be 14,000 million hectares in 2050. That is unless global warming and the consequent rise in sea level causes major flooding.

With a constantly increasing population, there will come a time when there are insufficient quantities of even the most basic resources such as water and if we are not careful, even fresh air could also be in short supply. Certainly the capacity for agriculture to keep expanding food production is very limited. Human population growth is, however, far less inhibited. The net result is that the greater the total global population, the lower will be the average standard of living.

Mankind has often had to cope with changing circumstances. Adjusting to one change will only lead us into a situation when we must cope with another. The difference is that change is no longer linear but is now exponential. We must learn to do the seemingly impossible. To change our expectations from growth and excessive consumption to a level of sustainability.

RELATIONSHIPS

Our ability to form, maintain and enjoy healthy relationships is the key to our happiness. A prerequisite to this is having developed a healthy relationship with ourselves. That is, liking the person we are and feeling that we are worthy of mutually caring relationships.

When we think about relationships, most of us, and certainly the young, tend to think of romantic relationships. We are, however, to a greater or lesser extent in relationship with every person with whom we come into contact. We are also in relationship with our environment. We affect and are affected by the place in which we live as well as the climatic conditions in which we live. For example, it is quite different living through a freezing cold winter in Chicago than living in a quiet, tropical, developing country.

For all of us, the first and most important relationship is with our family. Do we feel that we were and are loved by our family? Specifically, do we feel that our parents loved us? For most people, but by no means all, the answer to this question will be yes. Most people can be and are critical of their parents. Equally, however, most people who are lucky enough to have felt that they were loved, know that on balance their parents wanted the best for them.

There is also the issue that when we are in a position to do so, some of us either consciously or subconsciously, may re-write the history of our lives and our relationships. Selective memory may occur when looking through the cloudy lens of hindsight. Alternatively, we may deliberately choose to airbrush some of the imperfections of our past.

A writer who had researched many biographies said he had learned that the best source of accurate information about people were secondary sources. The closest source had usually told the story so frequently that over time it had become embellished and frequently distorted.

In adulthood, our relationship with living parents will vary for everyone. The first thing that has changed, or could change, is the power structure. The older we become the more independent we are, or should be, from our parents. The goal of any caring parent should be to produce children who are well prepared for life as an independent unit, whether singly or as a new family. That does not mean that at a particular age parents will wish to cast their children adrift. Nor does it mean that parents no longer wish to share in, guide and participate in their children's lives. In a healthy relationship, children would want to encourage and welcome a certain level of parental participation.

Problems arise when the timing and degree of independence sought by the children, and that considered appropriate by the parents, do not coincide. Every conscientious parent wishes to protect their offspring. One of the hardest things for parents is to see their children making what they as parents believe to be a mistake, without intervening. The very fact that parents are older than their children means that they do have more life experience and believe that they are better equipped to judge most situations. This despite the fact that each new generation will be growing up in a different environment and will certainly be faced with social and financial circumstances that were probably unknown to their parents.

It is both obvious and surprising that we are not clones of our parents and our children are not clones of us. People outside our immediate families often comment on how alike or different we are to our parents. The expression "a chip off the old block" may well have applied more in the past when our lives were so much simpler and may not have varied very much from generation to generation.

Even then, every child was in some way different. Beethoven was the ninth child of a syphilitic mother. Two of his older siblings were blind and another was mentally impaired. Just as individual children can achieve extraordinary greatness, so others can fail to reach the expectations which family or society may have had for them.

Many of the great European aristocratic families were founded by an individual with exceptional qualities, although these qualities were not always honourable. Many of the people who acquired great power and wealth did so through brutal and dishonest means. They were, nevertheless, exceptional in their own way, which is why they achieved what they did. There is a saying about rich families which suggests that the first generation makes the fortune, the second generation spends it and the third generation loses it. Although somewhat over-simplified, this highlights that different circumstances produce different drives and expectations in successive generations.

We all feel that we are living in a time of great challenges. There is uncertainty about peace in the Middle East, global warming, terrorism and a host of other issues. We are all living on the crest of the wave. It is about to break and we do not know what will happen after that. But so it has been through the ages. Everyone throughout time has lived on the crest of the wave. No one has ever known what the future would bring. There has always been fear and uncertainty. Only the object of our fear changes. A thousand years ago, people in Britain huddled inside small wooden stockades frightened of attacks by Viking invaders. A thousand years before that, the population lived in fear of a Roman invasion.

Meaningful relationships are formed as a result of time, circumstance and deliberate effort. Children are obviously influenced by their parents because it is with them that they spend the greatest amount of time and it is from them that they receive emotional support and guidance. As we grow older, with whom do we spend time and with whom do we share emotional support?

We form relationships in a variety of ways and for a variety of reasons. We all need to socialise and we therefore all need a social network which includes friends. We all have a place of employment and need to find a way of working in harmony with our work colleagues. After puberty, we are all influenced by our drive to find a sexual partner. We may have a variety of different relationship circles but it is also possible or even probable that there will be some overlap between these.

Successful relationships are mutually beneficial. At work, it is obviously theoretically best if we all treat each other with courtesy and co-operate as much as possible in order to get the job done. When we socialise, we want to feel that our company is valued by other people. When we are in a loving or sexual relationship, we want to feel that we have been chosen and we are loved because we are different and special.

If those are the things that we wish to receive from a relationship, it is more than likely that those are the same things which other people would like to receive in a relationship from us. In an ideal relationship, there should be a balance in which there is more or less equal giving and receiving. In friendship, or in any other relationship, the balance may well vary from time to time. If a friend is going through a difficult stage and needs our support, that is a time when we should give, rather than expect to receive.

Successful marriages, loving partnerships and close friendships vary enormously in their compositional makeup and appearance. They do, however, share one main ingredient. That is mutual caring. The most successful marriage that I know of worked because each partner constantly wanted the very best for the other. So each partner both gave and received the very best.

We all understand that casual friendships are picked up and then dropped according to our circumstances. For example, if we move into a different work environment we will by necessity associate with a different group of people. No one's life is static. As time passes, we literally and metaphorically travel to new places and are constantly exposed to new experiences. Each of us is in a constant process of maturing mentally and emotionally. A wise friend once said that he is not now the same person that he was 20 years ago. That must surely be true for all of us.

The problem that can occur in some long-term relationships, including marriages, is that people mature and change in different ways. So two people whose lives ran in parallel when they started the relationship could find their lives have become divergent. How often have we heard the expression that, he or she is not the same as when they first married. The Christian wedding service binds couples together with the requirement that only "death can cast them asunder," that only death can separate them. But these words were written when life was even more uncertain and when average life expectancy was only thirty or forty years.

Legal reform allowing the dissolution of marriages, combined with the extension of many useful years of healthy life, have led some people to move out of long-term relationships in order to explore new lifestyles, more suited to the person they have become. When relationships change or cease, including those changes caused by death, there is always pain and suffering. Usually one of the two partners will suffer more than the other. There is no avoiding the pain, but this beautiful, thought provoking and comforting piece by an unknown author may help:

To a special person – "Reason, Season or Lifetime"

People come into your life for a reason, a season or a lifetime. When you know which one it is, you will know exactly what to do.

When someone is in your life for a reason, it is usually to meet a need you have expressed outwardly or inwardly. They have come to assist you through a difficulty, to provide you with guidance and support, to aid you physically, emotionally or spiritually. They may seem like a godsend – and they are. They are there for the reason you need them to be. Then, without any wrongdoing on your part and possibly at an inconvenient time, this person will say or do something to bring the relationship to an end. Sometimes they die. Sometimes they walk away. Sometimes they act in such a way that they force you to take a stand.

What we must realise is that our need has been met, our desire fulfilled. Their work is done. The prayer you sent up has been answered and it is now time to move on.

When people come into your life for a season, it is because your turn has come to share, grow or learn. They may bring you an experience of peace or make you laugh. They may teach you something that you have never done before. They usually give you an unbelievable amount of joy. Believe it! It is real! But, only for a season.

Lifetime relationships teach you lifetime lessons, those things you must build upon in order to have a solid emotional foundation. Your job is to accept the lesson, the love and the person. To put what you have learnt to use in all other relationships, and all other areas of your life.

It is said that love is blind but friendship is seeing with understanding and compassion. Thank you for being a part of my life. May God hold you in the palm of His hand and Angels watch over you.

TOUCH

We all start life in the tight and warm confines of the womb. As a foetus, we are constantly in tight contact, touched, held and moved. After birth we are exposed to the cold and lose the sense of security which constantly being held had given us. No wonder so many cultures wrap babies tightly in swaddling clothes.

Physical touch is something that we all need throughout our lives. In normal loving families, infants and children are held, hugged and touched. It is the most natural and wonderful way in which to give and receive love. Young children still enjoying their innocence can, like puppies, tumble over each other and casually fall asleep against the warmth of another body.

Many studies have shown that touch deprivation leads to substantial psychological damage such as aggressive behaviour and even stunted growth. Children get a sense of being loved and wanted through physical touch long before they understand language and concepts. If we do not feel that we are loved as babies and children, our personality and character develops without the strong foundation provided by the sense of being wanted and loved.

There is the generally held belief that visiting the dentist is an unpleasant experience which is avoided by most people. One retired dentist said that he was aware that some of his female patients enjoyed their proximity to him. He sensed that these people needed to feel human closeness and that on occasions, in his role as a dentist, he had unintentionally provided fulfilment of this need.

The need for and desire for touch never leaves us. Our skin, all twenty square feet of it, is wonderfully sensitive. Throughout our lives it can be pleasurable and comforting to be touched and stroked. Without thinking about it or being conscious of it, we satisfy our deep seated sense of being loved when we are touched.

Receiving and giving massage, especially to a partner or lover, can be an extraordinarily wonderful experience. Our finger tips are a bundle of beautifully sensitive nerve endings. One of the most powerful positions is for the person giving the massage, to sit on the floor with their back to the wall. The person being massaged then sits between their legs lying back against them. In this position the giver can massage the scalp, face and upper body. The receiver feels enveloped and totally nurtured.

The trouble is that all the adults around us are sexual and we ourselves are sexual. Men especially often see touch, not as beautiful in its own right, but as a mere prelude to sex. Women in turn become suspicious of male touch because of its possible motivation or feeling that it may require sex as a follow up. The consequence is that parents and society in general become guarded and protective about touch. Innocent, loving and casual touch is increasingly treated as suspect. In our desire to protect our children from what is inappropriate, we deny them, and all adults, one of the most beautiful and natural forms of human interaction.

Touch is soothing, it reduces anxiety and gives us a sense that we are worthy of human connection. We all need touch and should not feel inhibited about seeking it out. We can hug members of our family. If it has not been traditional to do so, we can take the initiative to start physical contact. In this way we will be giving and receiving not only touch itself but also that most wonderful form of human connection, intimacy – into-me-you-see.

Different societies do have different codes of behaviour. All of us know what is acceptable or inappropriate behaviour within our social group. It is up to us to exercise the freedom we have within acceptable practices to touch and to be touched. Touching can and should be pleasurable for both people involved. Someone once asked if we give a hug, receive a hug or share a hug. The answer is that if we touch and hug with a sense of altruism and with the generosity of sharing a loving gift, as opposed to taking something solely for ourselves, we will probably not get it wrong.

Any of us who have ever had a family pet such as a dog or a cat will know the wonderful pleasure of stroking and patting the animal. It feels good to them and it feels good to us. We humans can also get a professional massage. People who are involved in bodywork believe in and completely understand the beneficial effects they are able to give. Therapists know that through touch the immune system can be strengthened. They offer relief from physical tension and the emotional stresses which caused it. Their touch has relaxing and rejuvenating qualities. For example, whether or not a person specifically believes in reflexology does not matter. Most people gain a wonderful sense of peace when their feet are gently manipulated.

I personally believe that the greatest gift we can give to our children, to our lovers, to the elderly, and to the dying is loving touch. Slow, rhythmic and gentle. To give them a sense of quietness and connection. To give them the comfort of release. To give them security through being touched and held, both physically and emotionally.

SEX

In the 1960s when Paul McCartney was in India practising transcendental meditation he saw two monkeys copulating in the middle of a road. A male simply jumped onto the back of a female, and to use his vernacular expression, "simply gave her one." Within a few seconds the whole affair was over. Pragmatism applied to procreation.

Samuel Johnson, referring to sex for us human beings, noted: "*The position is ridiculous and the pleasure is fleeting.*" Maybe Shirley MacLaine understood the human psyche better when she pointed out that for us, "*Sex is hardly ever just about sex.*"

Physical attraction for another human being is not something we plan, but it has certainly happened to all of us. We all know what it is like to continually want to look at the person we desire. We would like to touch, hold and caress that person and our greatest wish would be for them to reciprocate that desire.

Sex is one of the great human needs and yet it is unlike the others. In every culture, we know and accept the need to eat and sleep. We eat openly in public and there are no concerns about sleeping other than the fact that we are not supposed to do it when we should be doing something else.

Sex is undertaken in private. Most people, and especially the older generation, will never have seen anyone else performing (live) sex, nor will they have been seen undertaking sexual acts by anyone other than the people with whom they were engaging in sex. Most societies even go so far as to legislate that sexual acts must be undertaken in private. To do so in public is a criminal offence. The net result is that we hide much of our sexuality and are furtive in revealing this facet of our personalities.

In early Georgian England, most of the population freely engaged in whatever types of sex appealed to them and it was openly, uninhibitedly discussed. The Victorian era saw a huge pendulum swing away from what they considered to be the immorality of libertine living to erotophobia, which in turn led to the stifling and repression of sexuality. Indeed, the Victorians were so concerned with propriety that they even covered the legs of furniture to avoid any erotic connotation. In the guise of propriety, sexual ignorance was widespread.

There is the story of John Ruskin, the social theorist, who as a virginal bridegroom, was horrified to discover on his wedding night in 1846 that his bride had pubic hair. His biographer deduced that his only prior knowledge of female pudenda had come from marble statues which did not depict pubic hair.

Women were even more repressed than men at this time. The idea that a woman, or more specifically a lady, could enjoy her sexuality was deemed either impossible or inappropriate. Women were considered (by men?) to be non-sexual and certainly non-orgasmic. Throughout this time and well into the first half of the 20th century, the clitoris was almost unknown not only to men but also to vast numbers of women.

There is an apocryphal story from this era, called the "chloroform bride." It claims that on her wedding night a young, virginal, bride chloroformed herself into unconsciousness after leaving a note pinned to her dress saying that her bridegroom could now do with her as he pleased.

A counsellor was told by a client that when she was aged ten (in the 1970s), her mother informed her she was going to start kissing her daughter on the lips. This was to make her get used to the idea that she would have to "put up" with men doing this to her later and that she would have to pretend to enjoy it.

Where did this guilt, shame and ignorance come from? Christianity and especially Roman Catholicism believes in the concept of original sin. The concept that we are all tainted from birth by the knowledge and sexual sins of Adam and Eve. It is an ecclesiastical version of Napoleonic law in which we, like suspected criminals, start off from a position of guilt.

From puberty onwards, we are constantly aware of our sexual needs. We are surrounded and bombarded by sexual references and imagery. Films and some serious television dramas are increasingly explicit in the showing of fully nude sex scenes. They are totally realistic, except presumably for penetration. Naturally we respond to all of this sexual signposting, yet for many people there is no sexual outlet other than masturbation.

Why is it that masturbation as a subject for general conversation is still generally taboo. It is one of the pillars of schoolboy jokes – everyone accusing the others of "doing it" and yet denying that they themselves ever would.

The fact is numerous studies and surveys from Kinsey onwards repeatedly show the same thing. The vast majority of both men and women have found pleasure in self-stimulation of their genitals from early childhood well into old age.

Catherine Millet, known in France as "Madam Sex" because of her prodigious sexual experience, is an advocate of masturbation. She rightly points out that it gives each of us, but especially women, the ultimate control during sexual stimulation. Why therefore do we view such a natural and common practice as inappropriate and unspeakable? Why does society disapprove of a harmless activity which provides pleasure and relief?

The first known critical admonition of masturbation comes in the Bible with the statement that "Onan spilt his seed upon the ground." The humourist Dorothy Parker named her budgerigar "Onan" because he constantly spilt his seed.

Apart from masturbation, we require the involvement of another human being in order to participate in sex. This immediately opens the possibility to a range of emotions and actions from mutually loving to the self-centred, guilt-ridden and abusive. Why do so many of us engage in sex when what we are really seeking is intimacy? Perhaps it is because we are confusing the two separate, albeit interrelated, emotions of sexual gratification and intimacy. Caring, loving sexual connection can lead to the most beautiful intimacy, whereas quick sexual relief is merely genitally gratifying.

Why is it that society treats sex, one of our greatest needs, differently from other human needs? Why, for example, if we are all so sexual do we not invite friends round for a sex party as casually as we invite friends round for a dinner party? Why do we not have sex in front of each other as casually as we eat a sandwich or drink a cup of coffee? Why are we so censorious and judgmental? In ancient Rome and in 18th century Polynesia this is exactly what people did. Being openly and publicly sexual was completely normal in those societies.

The short answer is selfishness and control. All male creatures are programmed to pass on their genes, not to co-operate with and support others in being reproductively successful. Male lions will kill the cubs from a previous litter to ensure the best survival opportunity for their own offspring. Prior to the age of DNA testing, it was impossible to tell for certain who had fathered any child. In Judaism, you are only considered to be born Jewish if your mother was Jewish. In the Caribbean, there is a lovely expression which says "Mama's baby, Papa's maybe." Men want to know that the children they are feeding and supporting are genetically theirs. Historically, the only way that this could be done was by controlling the sexual activity of the women with whom they wished to enjoy sex and procreate.

When we humans are sexually attracted to someone, and more importantly when we are in a relationship with that person, we have a sense of possession and ownership. Our partner's sexuality and their body should belong to us and not be available to anyone else. This is not only a human trait, as we can readily see that many animals protect their sole right to be sexual with their mate. The concept of "survival of the fittest" includes the requirement that all animals urgently wish to pass on their own genes. Is it that we humans are still burdened by these innate impulses to the detriment of open sexual expression?

Throughout time, religious hierarchies have sought both to interpret what they thought was the will of God and also to consolidate the power and control they held as the interpreters of God's will. The net result is that all of the major religions have established firm rules for sexual conduct. Whether we as individuals are or are not religious, does not really matter. We are all swept along on the currents of social acceptability formed out of the religious dictates of the last few millennia.

If we are to make all our own decisions about how we wish to lead our life, sex is a good starting place. As adults, we have every right to decide what sort of sexual activity we wish to engage in, and with whom. Yet there are of course many barriers to complete sexual freedom. The first is that there may be vast numbers of people with whom we would like to have sex but that does not mean that they wish to have sex with us. So morally, ethically and legally, we are confined to having sex with adults who mutually consent.

Another important constraint in our society is that the majority of ongoing relationships imply or require monogamy. The Christian wedding vows include the phrase *"Keep thee only unto Him or Her."* Even if a couple are not religious, the assumption is that they will be monogamous. If they are not, they are considered to be "cheating" within the relationship. So are we irrevocably bound by the sexual norms which have developed over the centuries as a result of male and religious control?

Many books have been written claiming to have the solution to the greatest deterrent of monogamy. That is many authors outline practices designed to rekindle sexual desire in long-term relationships. My own feeling is that pure sexual desire does need an element of novelty which is almost impossible to simulate regardless of what games we play. Intimacy, however, is overall a greater prize and long-term pleasure than superficial sex alone.

Many societies have in the past and still do operate sexual

activity on a two tier system. In Oriental and African countries it is often the practice for a wealthy man to support a younger mistress while maintaining his wife and family. This allows the men to have sexual freedom without disrupting their family structure. The wife who is genuinely valued by the husband keeps her place in society and the financial benefits relating to this. London in the 19th century was very similar. Affluent men often maintained a mistress and the less affluent used the services of one of London's many bordellos. Some wives find it preferable for their husbands to have non-committal sex with a prostitute than to be engage in an affair which could pose some type of real threat to the marriage.

The French court went so far as to instigate the position of "official mistress." The king had an appropriate wife, who in turn produced legitimate heirs. Meanwhile the king chose a succession of sexual partners. Perhaps the most famous of these was Madame de Pompadour, the noted "official mistress" to Louis XV.

Today, statistics indicate that 60% of men will have some kind of sexual relationship outside their marriage. Researchers already know that very few people who divorce end up by marrying the person with whom they were having an affair. Having said that, Sir James Goldsmith noted that *"any man who marries his mistress immediately creates a vacancy."*

With gender equality in the West, women have also sought and participated in greater sexual freedom. Statistically, about 40% percent of married women in the United Kingdom will have sex with someone other than their husband during their marriage, and this percentage is thought to be on the increase. So, should we be asking the question, if both men and women want greater sexual freedom, that is to have sex outside marriage or the main relationship, should society recognise this change and allow it to take place in a spirit of openness?

Polyamorists are a small but burgeoning group already participating in a lifestyle which is well outside the social norm but which provides just such freedom. "Poly" meaning many and "amor" meaning love. Both men and women will be in relationships with more than one person. Usually conforming to their normal sexual orientation but sometimes extending to "bi-curiosity" or fully recognized bisexuality. The difference is that these relationships are conducted openly, honestly and with mutual consent. Either or both partners within a couple will additionally be in a sexual, and possibly loving, relationship with one or more other people.

It has been said that there are heterosexuals, homosexuals, bisexuals and trisexuals. The latter work on the basis that if it is sexual, they will try it. In reality, most humans are somewhere on a scale between being 100% heterosexual to 100% homosexual. Even predominantly heterosexual people have some attraction to members of their own gender. A small minority of people are genuinely non-sexual or asexual. Human sexuality is a complex, multi-dimensional issue and now there is ever more recognition of the fact that the brush stroke of heterosexuality has been smudged into ambi-sexuality loosely referred to as flex-sex or hetero-flexibility.

Courtship rituals keep changing or have been dispensed with all together, as in the current American campus practice of "hooking up" in which students openly and freely engage in sex without any pretence of starting or maintaining a relationship. Or is this merely a new name which legitimises the long-established, if somewhat disapproved of, practice of the "one night stand"? The boundaries of sexual prohibition may have expanded and changed. What does not change is the lure and excitement of errant behaviour which exceeds prevailing social conformity.

During the summer when I was 21, I lived in Canada in a fraternity house, an all male student residence. On one occasion, I briefly met a visitor to the house, a lovely young woman of about my own age. She was a British Cabinet Minister's daughter and a quintessential English Rose. Seemingly pure, modest and lovely, I was immediately smitten. About a month later I returned to the house late one evening to find all the other young men in a state of great excitement. The Cabinet Minister's daughter had been there and had initiated a sexual "free for all" with anyone who was there, welcome to join in.

Perhaps as an over-reaction to such behaviour, the American Purity Movement promotes total chastity, believing that we live in a sexually chaotic era. Young adherents to this movement pledge to remain non-sexual and usually non-physical until the day of their marriage.

As a boy of about 14, I remember being greatly agitated by the question of whether or not it was possible to be in love with two people at the same time. As an adult, I would view this somewhat differently. I would say that it is certainly possible to be in lust with two people at the same time; quite possibly many more than two. In terms of being in love, in the sense of being infatuated, I think that it is only possible to have this type of focus on one person. In terms of having a close loving bond which could include intimacy and sex, I do believe that it is possible for us to maintain this with more than one person at the same time.

Does this not in fact produce the greatest overall amount of happiness? This may seem like the ultimate "win-win" situation. We have some of our intellectual, emotional and physical needs satisfied by one person and others supplied by someone else. We in turn can share those special qualities which we possess with more than one person. Even polyamorists will say that life does not always work quite this smoothly. Inevitably, misunderstandings can arise. Moreover, just as the benefits and richness of their lives have expanded, so too have the complications, difficulties and responsibilities. Early exponents of polyamorism included Jean-Paul Sartre and Simone de Beauvoir, but even for them and for later practitioners such as Catherine Millet and her husband, the reality of jealousy marred the philosophical ideal of openness and freedom.

The Victorians cynically said that men accepted marriage in order to get sex and that women put up with sex in order to have marriage. Today a more enlightened but overlapping sentiment might say that men go through sex to intimacy and that women go through intimacy to sex.

While fully recognising women's desire and need for sex, there is little doubt that men's attitude towards and capacity for sex differs from that of women. Young men have the capacity to quickly masturbate to orgasm many times a day. As a result of inappropriate guilt about masturbation, most boys learn to masturbate clandestinely and quickly. This combined with the huge amounts of testosterone in young men frequently leads to premature ejaculation during actual sexual intercourse. As men move into their 30s and 40s, they are probably at their most sexually efficient. At this age, they can achieve and maintain strong erections and yet hold their own climax for as long as they want, for the benefit of both themselves and their partner.

Later in life, many men have difficulty in achieving a satisfactory erection. In his sixties, Geoffrey Barnard, known for "having lived a life full of fast women and slow horses," said that he did not believe in male impotence. His solution was to find a sufficiently attractive younger woman who would "turn him on."

In reality, the sexual tables do turn. Women can enjoy sexual intercourse, freed from the constraints of the monthly cycle and from any subconscious fears of pregnancy, while men of the same age may not be able to "perform." Many of those same men who were once sexually voracious now feel humbled by their inadequacy, frustrated by a mind which is still programmed to think that it wants frequent sex, and genitals which lie relatively dormant unless pharmaceutically assisted into action.

No discussion about sex would be complete without reference to both pornography and prostitution. Many of the arguments for or against both pornography and prostitution are the same. Historically, there has always been a global demand for, and the supply of both. Erotic paintings can still be seen on the walls of the beautifully preserved 2,000 year old brothel in Herculaneum.

There is also a middle ground on the sexual spectrum of eroticism which the majority of people find acceptable and interesting. An example of this would be Rodin's much reproduced statue depicting "The Kiss." This is sensual and exciting in that it shows a couple mutually enjoying love-making as opposed to engaging in raw sex. It attracts us because it is the ultimate prize, combining mutual caring and desire, which realistically we sense will lead to the passionate crescendo of sex.

Those parts of the body that are considered to be sexual or a sexual "turn on" have varied throughout time and from culture to culture. Japanese geishas are tightly bound within many yards of figure-obscuring kimonos. Their faces are painted white and their hair is severely tied. The only part of their unpainted body which is visible is the nape of their neck and it is this which becomes an area of sensuality. In some aboriginal groups, the women are permanently topless and in these societies the breasts may not be considered as sexual. In many African and middle eastern countries, men are sexually attracted to curvaceous women with well rounded buttocks which they consider to be voluptuous – the complete opposite of many in the West who consider the epitome of feminine beauty to be size zero.

We can also ask why is it that partial nudity is more exciting than total nudity? Catching a glimpse of what we are theoretically not supposed to see is more exciting than the openly revealed naked form, the illicit feeling that there is better still yet to come.

As Jerry Seinfeld said in "The Shoes":

"Looking at cleavage is like looking at the sun.
You daren't stare at it.
It's too risky.
You get a sense of it and then look away."

A case of mammary versus man.

Today "soft porn" and the social changes it has produced are ubiquitous. The Sun newspaper boasts that it created the acceptability of this genre with the introduction of topless models on Page 3. Publishing editors have long worked from the motto

"If in doubt, edit out." Now sexually confident, or sexually confused, "ladettes" everywhere work on the motto "If in doubt, get 'em out." Many young girls today live with the mind-numbing apprehension that sex, without emotion, is a commodity which they are expected to deliver.

Perhaps more surprising is the apparent u-turn in what young women appear to want. Many now express the opinion that they do not want a man to say that he cares for her, let alone say that he loves her. One woman indicated this succinctly when she said of her lover that she *wished he would cut out all that stuff and just get on with the sex.* How sad it would be to lose the excitement, heartache and bittersweet pleasure of romance.

Pornography has become ever more available, starting with the invention of mass printing, followed by photography, videotape and now the Internet. Sometimes referred to as a "pornucopia," there are thought to be over 100,000 sexually explicit sites on the Internet. There is even a debate about whether pornography has followed technical advances or has been instrumental in driving some of them forward. Whatever the answer, the fact is that pornography is widely available and widely used. Whether this is good or bad depends on our own viewpoint.

My own feeling is that, sadly and irrevocably, the pendulum has swung too far. Boys and girls as young as 13 and 14, willingly and unwillingly, see vast amounts of hard core pornography. This must affect their attitudes to and understanding of relationships. It diminishes the expression "making love" to a pallid anachronism.

The arguments against pornography and prostitution include very genuine concern for the women and men employed in these industries. It goes without saying that it is totally unacceptable for anyone to be forced into this type of work, let alone be subjected to any form of violence. There is also the grey area in which sex workers do undertake the work voluntarily but do so out of necessity rather than preference. This argument can also be used about a huge segment of society doing menial jobs they do not enjoy.

There are also some sex workers who have simply chosen this occupation because they find it preferable to, and more financially rewarding than any other occupation which is open to them. Then there is the reality that some women voluntarily use sex in various ways for their own advancement. Each of us can decide what name or label we wish to ascribe to such behaviour.

So the issue being discussed here is whether pornography and prostitution are useful and beneficial, or harmful and destructive, to the user. It could well be argued that they provide a safe sexual outlet for the sexually deprived and anyone who does not have an available sexual partner. Conversely, it could be argued that obtaining sexual relief through masturbation encouraged by pornography is, in the long-term, restrictive. The ease with which pornography and prostitution are available can result in people failing to pursue real human relationships.

It is also undeniable that human sexual interest covers a wide range of practices. Here each individual must decide what they like as well as what they feel is acceptable. It can also be argued that an individual can enjoy watching activities which are unacceptable to their partner and in so doing cause no harm. Again, it is worth repeating that if "actors" are willing to voluntarily engage in non harmful sexual activity they may well be providing a sexual outlet which in turn means that this activity will not be suggested to or forced on an unwilling partner.

The counter argument to this is that if we see any sexual activity repeatedly undertaken we may start to consider it to be normal, acceptable and even desirable. Undoubtedly, pornography has by default become the sex manual of our time. Despite the fact that, however imaginative we are, sex is a fairly repetitive process, pornography does certainly display the fullest possible sexual repertoire. The anti-pornography lobby says that this leads to abuse and violence. It may well be that those with a propensity for certain behaviour and violence are encouraged when they see it depicted. Others are of the opinion that it is unlikely to initiate those activities in people without a predilection for that type of behaviour.

Beyond an unwillingness or inability to find a partner, pornography can substantially separate sex from any type of meaningful and mutually comforting human interaction. Gentle and loving contact with another human being can be replaced by "scratch the itch" self-centred gratification – sexual partners reduced to little more than a collection of bodily appendages and orifices. Foreplay and post-coital affection eliminated, only to be replaced by an attitude of "come and go."

Another issue relating to pornography is that of comparison. An extremely beautiful and sensual woman asked her lover not to compare her with any woman he might have seen in a pornographic film. This woman had outstanding beauty and a wonderful figure. She was supremely feminine and an enthusiastic lover. On the scale of desirability, this woman was at the very top. Yet she felt threatened by the lack of inhibition, apparent enthusiasm and gymnastic antics of a few relatively undesirable and unattractive "porn stars."

Men may also feel threatened by pornography. Some men watching such films will feel that they are "less well endowed" than every other man on earth. What they fail to remember is that the primary requirement for a male porn performer is not his theatrical ability to deliver a Shakespearean soliloquy but the size of his love muscle.

As a corollary to this, it may well be that heterosexual men and women actually have more comparative knowledge about the genitalia of the opposite sex than they do of their own. One woman said of course she knew more about male genitalia because she had fondled and fellated many of them, whereas she had never closely examined another woman's vulva.

Paying for sex with another human being can cover a whole range of experiences from the furtive to the joyous, from the urgency of a mission that needs to be accomplished to the playful. Those who provide sex for money vary just as greatly. Sadly, the majority may well fall into the stereotypical group of the hardened and the addicted.

Increasingly, there is a small percentage of sex workers who see themselves as providing much needed social services. For example, they may provide experiences for people who are unsure about their sexual orientation and who have no other opportunities for experimentation. They see "clients" whom they get to know and with whom they hold supportive, if not deep or intellectual, conversations. They genuinely are a form of therapist specialising in emotional and physical needs, which society dismissively lumps together under the guilty banner of sex.

Paying for sex has always followed the social patterns of demand. Throughout history, garrison towns have for obvious reasons always attracted prostitutes. Across the Canadian prairies there is a string of towns which have women's names such as Rosetown and Hannah. These towns originated on the sites where there had been a workers' camp for the men who were building the TransCanada Railway and are named after one of the women who "serviced" them.

We use the term "red light district" for areas where sex can be purchased. This stems in part from the railway engineers' practice of leaving their red lanterns outside brothels, so that if a train needed to be moved, people knew where to find them. In ancient China, crimson lanterns made of paper and lit by a candle, were thought to be sensual and were hung outside the houses of courtesans.

Some men seek out what is referred to as a GFE. A "girlfriend experience" in which sex is interspersed with conversation and perhaps the enjoyment of a meal together. In this situation, the woman understands and briefly satisfies the man's underlying need for caring and intimacy, even if he himself is unaware of, or would deny that he has such a need.

The Sunday Times (Review section dated 13 January 2008) told the story of "a Polish husband who sneaked off to a brothel in Warsaw while his wife was at work, only to discover that that was where she was working. They are now divorcing after 14 years together."

Paying for sex has historically been a male prerogative, allowing men temporary sexual release until their hormonal capacitor re-charged and the whole process cycled again. Today that is still predominantly the case but increasingly women are enjoying the freedom to participate in casual, good-quality sex. Just like men, they are using escort agencies and also travelling to countries which provide "sex tourism" for women, such as the Caribbean and North Africa.

Women who have paid for sex vary greatly in their attitude towards this process. Some say that it has provided a new experience of raw sensuality. Others have used it as a stepping stone to restarting their sex life in preparation for a new relationship, usually after a period of closedown – a time of abstinence or sexual hibernation. Still others have been disappointed, feeling that a commercial arrangement cannot give them the validation they seek as women.

Denmark has strict laws targeting those people (men?) who pay for sex. In other countries, such as the Netherlands, much of the society does not see what all the fuss is about. They see nothing wrong with sex, regarding it as an absolutely normal human function and quite possibly indispensable to human health. They welcome and encourage the legalisation and de-stigmatisation of sex workers. In so doing, they believe that they give freedom and protection to sex workers and reduce many of the problems such as the trafficking of women and the associated violence.

The world's oldest profession will certainly continue long into the future. If it is ever eliminated, it will be because some form of pharmaceutical or technological innovation gives us greater pleasure and satisfaction than sex with another human being. Even then, the moral debate about appropriate sexual behaviour will no doubt continue.

If we say that someone has had many lovers during their lifetime, that is complimentary. They have on many occasions enjoyed the greatest intimacy and human connection possible. If, however, we say that someone has had sex with many partners that is quite different. They have merely participated in a physical pleasure in the same way that we can enjoy, or be disappointed by, eating a meal.

There is a difference between enjoying mutual sex with someone whom we know intimately and care about deeply and anonymous purely physical, selfish, sex. Most people will encounter both during their lifetime. Most people can decide for themselves at different stages of life which is the most valuable to them. It is worth taking the time to think about and understand what each of us wants sexually and what arouses us both in practice and in our fantasies.

The key issue is that sex can be an important part of lovemaking. Equally, however, sex can be purely physical and devoid of all but the most superficial acknowledgement for the sexual partner. The problem is that society, and we as individuals, try to tie all aspects of sexual practice together. In the process of controlling and binding our sexual practice, we control and bind ourselves. If we could completely separate our sexuality and sexual practice from our relationships, we would all find substantial new freedom. A new form of honesty would develop in all of our relationships if we did not live under the constraints of sexual inhibition and conformity.

Ideally, we should all be free to share and enjoy the most wonderful human experience of a mutually loving and mutually passionate relationship. Likewise, we should also be free to uninhibitedly explore and enjoy sexual activity devoid of any pretensions. That is to recognise our ability to enjoy sex for its own sake.

All of us need to find a balance between taking what we need sexually and giving to our partner (if we have one) what they want and need. Most important of all, we must ask ourselves if our sexual practices are in harmony with what we believe in our hearts to be appropriate and acceptable? This may or may not coincide with what society in general believes to be appropriate. The important thing for all of us is that we should enjoy our sexuality without hurting anyone else and without feeling inappropriate shame or guilt.

FIDELITY

Frederic Raphael jokingly wrote "*Your idea of fidelity is not having more than one man in bed at the same time.*"

What does fidelity mean to you?

When one man thinks about his own past lovers he does so with warmth and affection. They have played an important part in his life and that will never change. He remembers a comment made by one very beautiful woman for whom he cared deeply. After a truly loving night she said that she would keep that memory forever, in her "jewel box." Strangely and unpredictably the relationship ended painfully and suddenly a couple of months later. The memory will always remain in his jewel box and he hopes that it will remain in hers as well. We all want to reach the end of our lives with our jewel box overflowing with wonderful, albeit fading, memories.

An acquaintance is an extremely alluring and sensual woman who, at the age of 50, can still attract and seduce almost any human being that she wishes to. Despite her impressive record of amorous liaisons, she has never been in, or wanted, a monogamous relationship. She grew up in a commune where she received love from everyone around her. Her feeling is that fidelity is related to security, or rather the lack of feeling secure. She contends that through the contract of fidelity, most people seek the security that their lover will never leave them. The type of permanent, guaranteed security that a child looks for in a parent.

Many well-publicised celebrity weddings show the happy couple being greeted and congratulated by former lovers and spouses. Liz Hurley, and more importantly her husband, appeared to welcome Hugh Grant at their wedding. Perhaps it was down to the fact that there are some relationships which we know are completely over. However strong the sexual passion may have been and however many times it may have been rekindled, there comes a time when both members of a former relationship know that it is thoroughly and irrevocably extinguished. If they are lucky, what remains is friendship borne out of the shared memories and spectrum of emotions they lived through together.

Interestingly, the question only has significance if strong emotions are still involved. Meeting someone with whom we, or our partner, were only casually involved or if the relationship was in the distant past it is almost a non issue. It is as if that claim to attraction, attachment and affection is now so tenuous as to be irrelevant.

The issue about is trust. We cannot control another person physically and we certainly cannot control their emotions. Equally they cannot control us. Even in the most stable and loving relationships there will be private fantasies which could be considered as "mental infidelity." The French psychologist Maryse Vaillant wrote, *Everyone has a right to a private life within their private life.* She went on to say that none of us has to reveal whom we may be fantasising about when we make love.

The definition of infidelity is open to different interpretations. It need not be sexual and could include levels of intimacy and secrecy which we do not reveal to the person in our primary relationship.

Human nature is such that we often hunger after one elusive ingredient in the emotional mix of life. Like the still sexually interested wife whose husband has gone a bit "pipe and slippers" we yearn for a touch of excitement. We remember the good times and the happiness in past relationships forgetting why we are no longer in those relationships.

Trust extends to allowing and honouring other people's privacy. The right that we all have to actions and thoughts outside our relationship. The right to know that our correspondence, computer records, telephone call details and banking affairs are indeed private and should not be violated.

Fidelity comes from the word "fidere" which is the Latin for trust. We must not only have faith in our partner but, equally importantly, have trust and have faith in ourselves and our own ability to hold the affection of our partner. In so doing, we avoid the minefield of doubt and distrust.

PARTNER RELATIONSHIPS

In the 1880s when marriage normally followed courtship, Thomas Hardy wrote that, "*All romances end in marriage.*"

By partner relationships, I mean those relationships in which two people are drawn to each other by love and sexual attraction. Human beings have always wanted this type of special relationship and still do. A prominent psychoanalyst recently said that the malaise most often presented by patients in her office was the lack of intimacy. Both genders, but especially women, pack their lives with work and other activities until they can no longer hide and ignore the painful void left by a lack of intimacy.

Freudians talk about transference. They say that our first love affair was with the person who raised us. Whether that relationship was satisfactory or not, we continue to seek out and transfer some of the characteristics that were in that relationship into our adult love life. The problem, of course, is that if there were unsatisfactory aspects of our rearing, including various types of abuse, we may continue to reproduce that situation and have unsatisfactory relationships.

Though many animals pair up for a season and some animals pair for life, nature abounds with reproduction which results from isolated sexual contact devoid of emotion and ongoing connection. Human beings function on both levels. We can be sexually interested in a person but have no desire for anything other than coitus. The pendulum can of course, swing from hormonal self-interest to the point where we wish to give someone else everything which will make them happy. Among aristocrats in mediaeval Europe, the strange ideal of courtly love evolved. In this, the purity and honour of a woman was so valued that in theory the love was never "sullied" by consummation.

Today in Western societies we are free to choose whatever lifestyle we want, including the format and makeup of our relationships. The choices available to us range from living in virtual isolation, through freely engaging in frequent varietal sex, to living in a monogamous relationship. Of course, this statement is somewhat oversimplified in that most people encounter a range of relationships during their lives. Meeting someone while on holiday in an exotic location can certainly lead to infatuation. The chances are that in retrospect this would be described as a "summer fling" rather than the "real thing"

So what is "the real thing?" What is it that most people really want? I believe that, at some stage in life, most people would by choice be in a loving, intimate relationship. Remembering that intimacy means deep connection and is not a merely a euphemism for sex, they wish to be secure in the knowledge that another person loves them, wants them and wishes to entwine their lives together.

Stripped down to the core of the matter, this is a simple proposition. We all want to love and to be loved. We all want to feel that the love we receive is genuine and sincere. We all want to feel that the love we are receiving will be ongoing. When a partnership like this has been in existence for some time, it is possible for both partners to feel that they have the best connection in the world. Some would describe this as the closest of all possible relationships, and those who are more spiritual will refer to their partners as "soul mates."

The great passionate love stories of history and literature revolve around the young. For example, the youthful Romeo and the 13-year-old Juliet. That is because the young have physical freshness combined with the energy and urgency of youth. The desire to be in a loving relationship does, however, stay with us throughout our lives. Herein lies part of the problem. In seeking a relationship, many people have the wrong target in their sights. They equate sexual energy and physical desirability with love.

Both men and women who advertise in the newspapers or are involved in Internet dating constantly pursue physical beauty, often possessed by people younger than they are. In other words, whether they accept it or not, these people are putting sexual desirability at the top of their list. Additionally, if they themselves do not have the necessary characteristics to attract sexually desirable, younger people, they will be endlessly frustrated in their search.

Even those who do have the ability to attract physically desirable people also get locked into a cycle of disappointment and disillusionment. One example is a woman who has just passed her 40th birthday. She is attractive, outgoing and since her teens has dated attractive men. Now that her latest relationship has crumbled after a few months she is wondering why she does not have and cannot find a permanent relationship.

The answer is simple. She always dates the same kind of man, usually after meeting them in a club. They are interested in her because she exudes the idea that there is great sex on offer without any strings attached. She is attracted to them because they have great bodies and because… well, yes, they have great bodies. Nowhere in this equation is there any preparation for, or thought about, what qualities could lead to a long term relationship. She is aiming at the wrong targets.

We first learn how to form relationships in our childhood. What sort of role model did our parents provide? Were they stable, loving and openly affectionate with each other? Interestingly, this woman's mother still commends her 40-year-old daughter when she picks up attractive lounge lizards, while at the same time lamenting that she has no grandchildren. Failing to make the connection between appropriate choice and stability might appear to be a genetic defect but in this case is more likely to be a trait which was parentally taught.

A blind man once said that of course he understood the concept of beauty. He also said that other people's attitude to the beauty of the person he was with did register with and affect him.

But overall he felt he was liberated from the unnecessary distraction of what a person looked like. His main interest was in personality and the rapport he developed with that person.

Sometimes we drift into marriage or cohabitation simply because the relationship has been going on for a long time. Many people instinctively know that they are making a mistake and that things are not right. Even so, they go deeper or make additional commitment. To make a relationship work, we not only have to do certain things that are supportive and positive but have to avoid those which are damaging. Cynicism within a relationship drags heavily. Insecurity develops if we have the feeling that our partner does not find us lovable. The paranoia that says someone wants to be with us solely for sex or money. One embittered man lamented that he regarded marriage as an anachronism. For him, it was synonymous with fear, control and need.

The ultimate goal in relationship terms would be to have a partner with whom we are totally compatible, who is physically attractive to us and with whom we share a great sex life. In reality, very few, if any, people get 100% of everything they want. So anyone who is serious about wanting a meaningful ongoing relationship should be honest with themselves and write out a list of qualities which they want in a partner. At the same time, they should realistically appraise what they are willing and able to offer to someone else.

After writing out this list, it should then be put into a sequence of importance. The most important characteristic they are looking for in a relationship should be put at the top of the list. My question and response list would be something like this.

What qualities and characteristics do I want in a relationship partner?

Compatibility
Companionship
Good communication
Openness

Honesty
Interesting conversation
Integrity
Reliability
Physical attractiveness
Sense of humour
Sexual compatibility

Everyone's list will have some of the components above as well as additions. Other lists will also be in a different sequence, but it is worth noting that sex does not have to be at the top of the list. After all, how much of our time do we actually spend engaging in sex? We spend a lot more time talking, preparing food in the kitchen and sitting in the car together. If we are not compatible on these occasions, there is very little hope of developing lasting happiness in the relationship.

Sex is the big trap. We become so preoccupied with it, that it overwhelms almost everything else. It can diminish to obscurity the importance of what matters most in a relationship – wanting to be with someone and enjoying their company while living our ordinary day-to-day lives.

Being "in love" is the other big trap. There is a huge difference between the wonderful, hormonally driven urgency of desire and the solid day-to-day caring about someone. However the relationship may start, we do not remain "in love" indefinitely. We can, however, sustain a wonderful loving relationship throughout our lives.

A good example of this is the French philosopher Andre Gorz and his British-born wife Dorine. In a 75 page essay, he outlined the enthralling love that they shared for 60 years. He used beautiful expressions such as "*You've given me all of your life and all of you. I want to be able to give you all of me in all the time we have left.*" Their lives were so entwined that neither wished to live without the other. In September 2007 they chose to end their lives together.

Drawing up a list like the one mentioned may seem similar to deciding what features you want when you purchase a new car. The big difference is that inanimate objects are there solely to serve us. In a relationship, it is obvious that our partner is going to want and need things from us. Whether or not they have ever actually written them down, our partner will also have a list of qualities which he or she will require in us in order to find us compatible.

So if, for example, we consider reliability to be an important quality and we find someone who is reliable we should ask ourselves if we in turn could be considered reliable. It is not a requirement that we should have identical characteristics to our partner. Sometimes little differences or foibles can be considered delightful or charming, but on major issues there must be a reasonable level of similarity.

People who sit around day-dreaming of their ideal partner usually focus on what they will receive; the benefits they will get out of a relationship. Already, they are visualising a one-sided relationship. The point is that relationships are just as much about giving as receiving. When we really care about someone, we want them to be happy and will gladly do whatever we reasonably can to make them happy. We will frequently put their needs before our wants and even put their wants before our needs. We are willing to give them time and attention rather than focusing on ourselves. This often involves some very unromantic and prosaic things. It means that we will be supportive in a variety of ways, from listening when they need to be heard, to doing domestic chores.

We can break down the concept of relationship into two words – relation and ship. The relation is the person to whom we are connected and the ship is the vessel in which we travel together. By definition, a ship is a large vessel and by inference it can withstand the open seas and heavy storms. Metaphorically, many of our relationships are conducted in much smaller vessels. We may be bobbing around in a small, over-loaded dingy which is fine for calm inland waters but useless on troubled seas. We may be in a speedboat which is exciting for short trips but not much good for the long haul. Even if we are in a large ship, we have to be careful it is not a destroyer or a battleship.

Being in a relationship does not mean that the person we are should be consumed or subsumed. What we really want is to connect with another person without losing ourselves. As single people, we all think of ourselves as being a complete unit. So when we go into a relationship we should not suddenly become a mere 50% of something. Rather, the whole relationship should be greater than the sum of its parts, like colourless water droplets combining with sunshine to produce a rainbow.

The wonderful Ukrainian dance known as "hopak" is a celebration of this. The fast-stepping movement opens with men and women dancing energetically together. They then part to celebrate the supreme beauty and femininity of the women. After dancing together again, they once more separate, this time to allow the men to display their machismo through their spectacular, testosterone-fuelled Cossack leaps. It is truly a celebration of the gender differences and the sheer joy they produce in coming together.

A healthy relationship also needs space and freedom. It is wonderful to have a partner with whom to do things but it is also important not to stifle each other. In the healthiest relationships, each partner is free to move in their own circles, pursuing their own interests, and in so doing brings freshness to their conversation.

When we are in a relationship we should focus on making that relationship work. We should forgive quickly and kiss slowly. We should not keep looking over our partner's shoulder for a more desirable person or situation. This is the true meaning of commitment.

Most people who are looking for a long-term relationship would do well to focus on the three Cs – compatibility, companionship and communication. We do need to communicate in all relationships. We need to communicate at work and we need to communicate in all our functional relationships such as dealing with shops, utility companies and the government. Most of all, we need to communicate with people who are closest to us such as our partner.

The more we get to know someone the greater is our ability to interpret what they are thinking. Couples who have been together for many years feel that they intuitively know what the other is thinking and how they will react to certain situations. This is comforting in some ways but runs the risk of diminishing actual conversation and removing the opportunity for fresh thoughts and ideas to be discussed.

When coming together, we must have the courage to use the newness of the relationship to establish and ensure open and clear communication. We must be open to hearing what our partner believes, perceives, thinks and wants. We must also take this opportunity to show who we really are. We too, have needs and desires, and we also have the right to reveal these.

As important as talking about what we want is having the courage to state clearly what we do not want. In a non-threatening or combative way, we must clearly and firmly identify our boundaries and say what is or is not acceptable for us. How we communicate is very important. All of us must resist the temptation to exaggerate and be overly dramatic. Soap operas on television show all of their characters grossly over reacting to even the most insignificant situations. That is how they create a "drama" out of even the thinnest storyline. Unfortunately, whole generations are learning their life skills from these frequently inappropriate role models.

The key to successful communication is doing it with sincerity and honesty. For example, when a couple come together and start to become sexual, it is in the best interests of both of them if they can openly discuss what they like and what they do not like. If we can trust someone to say no, in circumstances with which they do not agree, we can also feel comfortable that they have been truthful when they say yes and are in agreement. This way there is no misunderstanding. If we can discuss our sexuality openly in a way which is not threatening and hear what is being said without taking offence, there is every opportunity for us to become sexually compatible. Once open communication has been established, it should be maintained through regular dialogue. It's a bit like having an ear pierced. If earrings are not used, the opening will close over and be lost.

Through open communication, we find out whether or not we are compatible, not just sexually but in every way. Our compatibility will then affect our ability to enjoy companionship, which is the cornerstone of a successful relationship. Part of our communication can include humour. One young woman said recently that she was really pleased to be married. Now, she joked, she had someone special to annoy for the rest of her life.

Marital bliss is high in demand but somewhat short in supply. Unlike the purchase of consumer products, there is no easy way to return a spouse if not completely satisfied. Despite the high percentage of marriage and partnership break-ups, the prize of a good relationship is so desirable that most of us pursue it at some time.

Percy Shelly expressed this view most eloquently when he said

"Nothing in the world is single
All things by law divine
In one spirit mix and mingle
Why not I with thine?"

FINDING THAT RELATIONSHIP

There is no doubt that life in a relationship is different to life as a single person. There are advantages and disadvantages to both. Human nature is such that whichever state we are in, we spend a lot of time envying the benefits of the other.

Being single gives us a huge amount of freedom. We can come and go as we please. We can do whatever interests us whenever we feel like doing it and most importantly of all, we can choose without debate which TV channel we will watch. Conversely, there may be times, regardless of how many friends we have, when we feel lonely and even isolated. We also have to stay incredibly active in order to maintain our social life. There is endless planning about what we will do next weekend and with whom.

Being married or in a long-term relationship usually provides a level of stability and comfort. There is always someone to talk to and always someone with whom we can plan activities and the next holiday. A loving partner shares in our happiness and provides support in times of difficulty. There is the lovely saying that happiness shared increases and when sorrows are shared they diminish. The price we pay for these privileges and benefits is the requirement to give consideration to the needs and preferences of someone else.

We are all motivated to pursue those situations which attract us and to avoid those which we do not want. If we want to be in a relationship, is it because we want to give and receive those special benefits associated with having a partner, or is it because the prospect of remaining single frightens us? The thought that loneliness is the worst emotional state we can be in?

If we decide that we want to be in a relationship, how will we find that special person? Part of the problem lies right there in the expression "special person." After all, what is a mere stone to one person may be a gem to another. We are probably not looking for a person who is considered to be special by the rest of the world. We are looking for a person with whom we are compatible and with whom we can develop a relationship of mutual respect and love. We should be looking for someone who has the same aspirations and wants the same things in life that we want.

There is a tendency for young people to slip into and out of relationships of varying intensity. This is rightly a time of experimentation, a time of mild infatuations and intense feelings of love. Most importantly, this is a time when each individual can learn the process of relating to someone else, as being one half of a couple.

All of us have probably felt at sometime that there had been a long "arid" period between relationships. Then when someone comes along we rush to make it work. The problem is that the more urgent our desire to find a partner, the greater is the risk that we will try to force ourselves and someone else into a relationship which is doomed not to succeed. Some people live their lives with the attitude that even a bad relationship is better than no relationship at all. Despite suffering the repeated agony of relationship break-ups, it does give them a sense of being an active player in the world of romance.

New relationships all start with a sense of euphoria. The trouble is that euphoria, by its very nature, is not only addictive but also ephemeral. Marlena Dietrich, with her husky, seductive voice, famously sang, "Falling in Love Again," with the emphasis on "again." It takes courage to say to ourselves that, if we want a long-term relationship, we will act more cautiously and work at getting it right.

Myths and fairytales have left us with the belief that there is just "one special person" in the world who is right for us. If we search in the right places, kill enough dragons or kiss enough frogs, we will find them. In reality, there are hundreds and thousands of people in this world with whom we could share a loving relationship. In great swathes of the world marriage is arranged by families and professional matchmakers. This system may not have the hormonally fuelled excitement that is endlessly depicted by Hollywood. It does, however, have the practicality of going directly to the list of "most important" characteristics outlined in the last section.

We can be open to both systems. We can temper our first, usually sexual, attraction to someone by undertaking a realistic evaluation of compatibility. We can also think about prospective candidates while openly understanding that love can and does grow between two people who both want this to happen.

In other words, loving relationships are created and fostered by us, not pre-ordained by destiny. If we look in the right places, are realistic about our goals and expectations, and are willing to give as well as receive, there is a loving relationship available to all of us.

In purely practical terms, it is worth developing a spirit of openness by considering everyone we meet to be attractive and available. If we ourselves are easily approachable, people will indeed approach us, and it is possible that one of these approaches will lead to the sort of relationship we want.

If, like an increasing number of people, we turn to Internet dating or newspaper advertising, we should at least inject some humour into this process. One advertisement read, "*Man with chess board sought by woman with chequered past.*"

Another said, "*I am choosey but not desperate. Seeking a non-combative, emotionally stable woman, who is not being stalked, sued or medicated. Better still, if you are irresistible to most men but incredibly not currently selected ...*"

Under the heading of occupation one man wrote, "*Drug dealer and money launderer – also part time mafia hit man. Plus I do some creative writing. Hope you guessed the last bit!*"

Another advertisement said, "*Custer's last stand. Ageing*

Lothario shortly to be donating his prostate to medical science, seeks final fling with sympathetic, mature lady."

The mayor of a remote mining town in Australia with a substantial over-abundance of men advertised for single women. One local woman in the town commented on this by advising prospective incomers that *"the odds were very good but that the goods were also very odd."*

Finally, one amusing advertisement stated that, *"I have the body of Albert Einstein and the brain of David Beckham. Or should that be the other way 'round?"*

That brings us next to the question, our ever evolving personality.

LEVEL 4 - ESTEEM NEEDS

Achievement, status, responsibility, reputation

THE NEED FOR RECOGNITION

In East Africa, there is a lovely greeting which is used by some people. On meeting, one man will say to another, "I see you". To which the reply is, "I am here to be seen".

Not to be seen means that we do not count. The journalist, Ariel Leve, said that she had been to a couple of red carpet events in New York. On one occasion, she overheard a photographer ask a woman with a clipboard who she was. "No-one" was the reply. Surely that is the ultimate putdown. Human nature is such that even if we have no desire to be famous, we certainly do not wish to be invisible.

As human beings, we do wish to be seen and we do wish to be heard. We want people to notice us and to listen to what we have to say. This is true in our family environment, our workplace and in our various social contacts. The degree of recognition towards us by others indicates to us what value we are to them.

If that is true for us, it is also true for other people. Everyone wants some acknowledgement. It takes very little effort on our part to give that acknowledgement to other people. Simply making eye contact, smiling, or giving some simple positive comment. Even more amazing is that when we do this people usually mirror our attitude and respond to us in the same way. That is, if we have smiled at them they will probably smile back at us. How much more worthwhile than ignoring or scowling at people only to have them ignore us or scowl back!

RELEASING AND DEVELOPING OUR TRUE PERSONALITY

The philosopher Soren Kierkegaard said, "*Life must be understood backwards but lived forwards.*"

Throughout my teenage years, I suffered from shyness. This took the form of frequent embarrassment in most social situations. Specifically, I would become tongue tied and would often blush. To compound this, very annoying and unhelpful people would draw attention to my blushing. As my expectation of myself was to become tongue tied and blush, this became a self-perpetuating situation. Defining ourselves in this way is very damaging because it is likely to prevent our ability to change.

I certainly did not like this aspect of myself but did not know how to change. It seemed to me that other people were blessed with innate confidence and social skills that I did not possess. I envied those people who came from families in which the expectation was to be gregarious and socially at ease. I envied those people who appeared to be naturally witty and had the confidence to use humour.

The good news is that with time, I overcame the majority of these problems. How did I do this? Well it actually took me quite a long time, but I know that with the proper guidance and direction this can be achieved reasonably quickly. So here are some things to think about.

Shyness is a form of embarrassment which we feel in some situations that do not warrant bona fide embarrassment. Introversion is the state of mind in which a person is constantly introspective and looking inwards. In essence, embarrassment occurs when we are not comfortable with the truth, or more specifically with our perception of the situation. In my case, my perception of the truth was that I had nothing to offer. That I had nothing to say, which could be of any interest, to anyone else. Worse still was my feeling that I would say something foolish and so reinforce everyone's belief that I was a dim-wit.

The net result was that I lived up to my expectations of myself. When someone is insecure (or confident) it is quickly sensed by everyone around them. The feedback we then get from other people reinforces our own self- belief. With shyness, this is the negative cycle which must be broken by anyone who wishes to have the happiness of mixing easily in social or business situations.

So how did things change for me? At the age of 20 I left the UK to work and travel in the United States where I was lucky enough to find a job at the New York World's Fair. There were many other people of my age working there and many of them were also away from home. Although not deliberately planned, I now found that I was with people who knew nothing about me and they did not think of me as being socially inept. In fact, there was a certain benefit in America to speaking with an English accent; it was almost assumed that I was polished and intelligent.

As that was how others saw me, that became the role I adopted. The people I was mixing with probably had just as many insecurities as me. Nevertheless, we all had the need to work together, as well as a huge youthful desire to have fun. Looking back, I see this as the turning point in my life. I was no longer constrained by the gloomy predictions of my parents and teachers. I could now decide what sort of person I wanted to be, I could set my own course into the future.

A key factor in overcoming shyness is to stop thinking constantly about ourselves. To stop dwelling on how we think the world is viewing us. The more we look outwards and focus on other people the less we think about ourselves and the less we feel shy. If we focus our attention on other people we find that they enjoy this and are probably more receptive to us. Here again, we may need to move away from parental influence, especially if in childhood our attention was constantly being drawn towards our own behaviour and apparent failings.

My shyness did not evaporate over night, but I did start to see myself differently. I was not instantly imbued with confidence but I did develop the belief that I could cope in new situations. This belief was enhanced and consolidated through taking some social risks as well as the trial and error process which stretched my boundaries.

I was lucky enough to form a close friendship with a man a couple of years older than me. Frank was an attractive, outgoing young man with a great sense of humour. His Italian parents ran a bar and he had been used to mingling with many different types of people throughout his childhood. He had learned not to take the comments of inebriated customers personally. He had developed the art of light banter and had the ability to come out with amusing responses. In short, he had the ability to be at ease with people.

Frank and I were very different. Our backgrounds were poles apart and our experiences in life, such as the culture in the schools which we had attended, could have kept us apart. Even physically, we were completely different. Frank was short and dark, while I was tall and fair. But I recognised that Frank had some qualities and skills which I admired and envied.

Looking back after all these years, I realise that one of the skills I subconsciously learnt from Frank was to smile. When people spoke to him, almost regardless of what they said, he would smile. Not only would his face light up but his whole physical demeanour became expressive. His style was to be jovial and light-hearted. He may have developed this aspect of his personality when waiting on tables in his father's bar, but it was a good way to engage with people in almost any situation.

It was never my intention to become a Frank clone but I observed how comfortable he was with people and I tried to be the same. Just because my childhood had been constrained by a stuffy English upbringing did not mean that I could not learn a valuable lesson from an ebullient, Italian-American. What it did require was an acknowledgement that I was not happy with my ability to interact with people; an acknowledgement that I could see a better role model than I had come across before and a willingness to try something different.

We are surrounded by potential role models. Different people we meet, or characters we see on television, will have different sets of social skills. While we should be careful not to keep changing the target, it is worth deciding which personality characteristic we would like to change and the direction in which we would like it to move. We can then consciously and slowly move in the direction of change which we want.

So perhaps this is the first lesson. If we wish to change, we must somehow break the cycle of behaviour and expectation. This does not mean that we have to move to another country. It could, however, be desirable to start mixing with a completely different set of people – maybe moving out of the family home or changing jobs and choosing to mix with a different set of friends. If we do this, we must at the same time change our behaviour and our own expectations of other people's reaction to us. If we do not change, we will probably be treated in the same way as we were before.

There are also ways in which it is possible to facilitate and speed up change in the beliefs we have about ourselves and our behaviour patterns. Reading "personal development" books is a great way to start. Some doctors are now recommending such books in a practice referred to as "bibliotherapy." There is so much wisdom and guidance in these books. Look through the appropriate section of any good bookstore and you will find an abundance of titles from which to choose. Not all of them are will be relevant. In fact, not all of any particular book will necessarily be relevant, but almost certainly there will be sections which provide support, comfort and inspiration.

There are self-help CDs which are an inexpensive way to absorb positive messages. Listened to on a regular basis, they can be truly beneficial in changing our self-beliefs. They can help us to re-program our own reaction in certain situations. Similarly, there are books about auto-hypnosis and visualisation. On their own or in conjunction with CDs, these can be very helpful in understanding why we act in certain ways, such as blushing and how this reactive behaviour can be changed.

Help is also available in the form of community counselling, possibly involving Cognitive Behavioural Therapy (CBT) and hypnosis. The latter is particularly effective and works quickly. In my opinion, however, the actual method of change is probably less significant than the desire to change and the active pursuit of change.

FEAR, FRUSTRATION AND ANGER

An ideal world for any of us would be to have things exactly the way we want them. As an example from the animal kingdom, a herd of deer would no doubt be happy to graze in peace. The problem for deer is that there are numerous predators ranging from wild animals to man wanting to eat them. In their society, a structure has developed which means that only the strongest male gets to reproduce and he has to go through bloody fights in order to win that right. So even a deer's life has to contend with the issues of getting enough to eat, staying out of danger and trying to reproduce.

Assuming that we consider mankind to be the pinnacle of the animal kingdom, we are in a far more complicated position. Our language, ability to communicate, and think, gives us huge advantages and many pleasures but in turn allow us to feel and suffer from negative emotions such as fear, frustration and anger.

Our ultimate fear is death and instinctively we seek to preserve our own lives. We also fear lesser forms of harm, such as being physically damaged. Rightly we fear this, because it in turn could affect the functioning of our lives and may also be painful. The problem is that most human beings manage to feel fear about many situations which are not physically dangerous. We may feel fear if we think of that our job is threatened. (Perhaps in some ways this is understandable because it is a subconscious extension of our fear of starvation.) We may feel fear in some social interactions such as trying to attract a mate if there is another suitor whom we perceive to be stronger. We may feel that we are entering into a fight in which we will be hurt. The difference is that in all likelihood we will only be hurt emotionally, not physically.

The solution, which is easier said than done, is to put things into perspective. Every time we feel afraid we should ask ourselves to evaluate the real level of danger. What is the worst that can happen? If it involves a non-physical activity, we can immediately rule out the danger of death or physical harm. For example, if we have been asked to make a presentation at work, the worst thing that can happen is that we will not know what to say and that we end up looking foolish. The first thing is that we should consciously try to control our emotions so that our body is not unnecessarily flooded with adrenaline and cortisone

Continuing with the example of being asked to give a presentation at work, if we know in advance that this is going to happen, we can prepare for it. We can learn as much as possible about what it is we have to discuss and then practice giving the presentation. We could use visualisation to see ourselves speaking clearly and providing the information that is required. If we have no time to prepare we must at least be psychologically ready.

That is we must remain calm and think about how we can respond. We must not fall into the trap of thinking about all the things which we do not know or cannot do. One of the best ways to think about this is to respond as if a friend had asked you the same question. You will then talk about what you know and what you think. The fear is eliminated when you cease to put increased value on the circumstances. In other words, do not create a fearful situation for yourself.

In her wonderful book, "Feel the Fear and Do It Anyway" Susan Jeffers refers to studies which show that 90% of what we worry about never actually occurs. She goes on to say, "*Pushing through fear is less frightening than living with the underlying fear that comes from a feeling of helplessness.*" How very true that is. Fear itself can be more debilitating and damaging than the occurrence about which we are afraid.

Another debilitating emotion is that of frustration. We become frustrated when the action we want to take place is blocked. Frustration is real and may have very important underlying causes. For example, a national government may be frustrated by its inability to change the human rights behaviour of another democratically elected government. On an individual level, we may be frustrated by the fact that someone whom we love does not reciprocate that love. Mostly, however, frustrations are relatively small: we are annoyed by the queue in the bank, slow-moving traffic or our teenage son's unwillingness to keep his bedroom tidy.

However great or small our frustration, the fact remains that frustration itself is a damaging negative emotion. Petty frustration can grow into anger and can cause us to loose our temper and move into a state in which we no longer think logically. It drains our energy without achieving useful results. It is possible and even probable that frustration will cause us to take the wrong course of action. Some years ago I became increasingly frustrated in my dealings with an insurance company. It seemed to me that no one was actually reading my letters and no one cared enough to find an appropriate solution.

I remember writing an absolutely blistering letter to an insurance company. It was a masterpiece of sarcasm and scorn. It was so strong that I became concerned that I could end up in legal trouble for writing it. A wise old friend and mentor happened to be a retired lawyer, so I asked him what he thought of the letter. He read through it carefully and without smiling commented on the fact that I had indeed written a powerful, emotional and highly critical letter. Then he asked me one simple question. *"What exactly are you trying to achieve?"*

My first reaction was to act with frustration towards him as well. After all, I was asking for his legal opinion as to whether or not I could be sued for writing such a letter, not an opinion on the merits of my insurance claim. Calmly he went on to explain that my letter would be sure to infuriate the reader. Good, I thought, that is what I want! But he said that infuriating the reader was likely to cause them to be even less co-operative than they had been in the past. He told me that I could not be sued for sending the letter and that I was completely free to do so. He did, however, suggest that I should not mail the letter until I had given the matter further thought.

On reflection, as a result of my frustration, I realised that my letter was designed to score points and make me feel good. My right to be assertive had changed into an aggressive attack. Konrad Lorenz in his book, "On Aggression" pointed out that we can readily understand that animals have to fight their prey and their enemies in order to obtain food and save themselves from becoming the food of others. He was also quick to point out that aggression is totally different from predation. He gives the example of a man viewing a turkey which he is about to kill and eat. The man feels no aggression towards the bird. His emotions are in no way aroused. He simply understands that he must have food to survive. The emotion of aggression is reserved by all animals for their own species in such matters as mating and territorial ownership.

My letter writing was a long way off the target of getting my insurance claim settled, so in a much cooler mood I re-wrote the letter. The basic argument was every bit as strong. What had been removed was the senseless and ineffective personal attack to which I had resorted out of frustration. The barrister and writer, the late Sir John Mortimer, said that *"the secret of cross examination was not to examine crossly."*

On this occasion, I was lucky in many ways. First of all, time and distance prevented the damage being done in the same way as if I had said the same things during a meeting or telephone conversation. Secondly, I had the wise counsel of a good friend. Most valuable of all were the lessons that I learnt from this – not to be distracted from the goal I am actually trying to achieve and not to exacerbate the situation through bad judgment. To remember that frustration is damaging and not helpful and to be aware of the fact that, while I cannot always ask my friend for his advice, I can remember his wisdom and think about what he would say to me.

Frustration often leads to anger. The angrier we become the less we are in control. There is the expression "being beside yourself with rage." It is as if there is a second person there who does not truly represent you. It is like driving fast. We may think we will get there more quickly but often we are only on the edge of control and sometimes lose it completely. The only reason for us to become angry is if we do not get what we want. Surely all of us realise that we cannot have everything we want all the time? There are many occasions on which we have the right to achieve our goals. On these occasions, the best solution is to act assertively but without anger. On other occasions, we should realise that we do not have the right to achieve the goal we want and that getting angry does not make our desire morally correct.

We will probably never eliminate anger and frustration from our lives. We can, however, endeavour to minimise them. We can do this by recognising our own reaction to various situations and by controlling our own build up of emotion. It is in our own interests to identify and manage our tendency to fear, frustration and anger. No one inflicts these emotions on us. Other people may control the environment which causes us to feel this way but it is we who actually choose our response. We can decide for ourselves how effectively we will control these negative emotions.

BEING ASSERTIVE

Assertiveness is when you stand up for your rights in a firm, calm and considerate way. Aggressiveness is when you demand your way, regardless of anyone else or any other issues involved.

In order to have self-respect and to have the respect of others, we must be effective. Put another way, we must feel that we can affect situations. Equally importantly, people around us must be aware that we have sufficient self-respect and confidence to ensure that our needs and views are respected and given full consideration. The opposite of this is to be powerless and have no control over any situation. Other people not only see this but will frequently use it to have control over us. Assertiveness, therefore, means that we retain an appropriate level of control over those situations in which we have a legitimate right to do so.

In order to have control, we must be assertive. We are all assertive in many ways every single day of our lives. We make decisions and carry out the necessary actions to be effective. For example, we are being assertive when we decide we want a cup of tea and take the action of putting on the kettle. Assertiveness only becomes an issue for us and for others when the action it is proposing comes into conflict with someone else's wishes.

Like most things in life, there is a need for balance and compromise. Here it is very important to realise that compromise does not mean merely giving in to another person's wishes. What it does mean is finding a workable solution, finding a balance between our rights and those of the other person. It does mean giving respect as well as receiving it.

Let me give a simple example which can be seen from both

points of view. Suppose you are driving down a slip road in order to join a motorway. You wish to join the motorway traffic and have every right to do so. Vehicles already on the motorway have every right to be there and to continue travelling on their journeys.

So you both have rights. But it is in both your interests to find a workable solution to be cooperative. Why? For a number of reasons. First of all, there are safety issues. If we do not co-operate, there is the possibility of an accident. As the person wanting to join the motorway, it is our responsibility to do so safely. Having said that, we must be sufficiently assertive to join a stream of traffic. Similarly, cars already travelling on the motorway understand that other traffic wishes to join. They can be selfish and maintain their speed, or they can be considerate and allow us to enter.

As in many situations in life, we see that there is an imbalance in the power structure here. In turn, we also see that there is a need both to be assertive and conciliatory. If it became standard practice that cars already on the motorway were always intolerant of vehicles joining the traffic, the intolerant drivers would also find it impossible to join the motorway when they wished to do so.

The first thing to remember is that we all have rights. What those rights are depend entirely on the situation in which we find ourselves. If we know that we are going into a situation of potential conflict, it is worth thinking about what our rights are. Some situations are fairly clear. For example, if we are returning a product to a store, we probably know the store policy about returns such as whether or not a product has been removed from the packaging. So, assuming we have abided by those rules, we are in a strong position to assert our right to return the product.

What is important in this example is that we go into the store knowing what we want and come out having achieved a fair and correct result. By that I mean if we wanted our money back and that is what we were entitled to, that is what we got. Not a replacement product or credit note or any other solution which was not completely satisfactory to us.

The real problem is that in most situations we do not have the opportunity to pre-plan how we will react. Moreover, the vast majority of situations do not have firm guidelines in place. Many of our interactions with other people are spontaneous and we cannot therefore plan specifically for them. But what we can and must remember is that we do have rights. In any given situation, it may be appropriate to pause. Yes, pause and ask ourselves, what are our rights in this situation? What is an appropriate way to respond in this situation?

An example of this could be that your mother phones and says that she is expecting you to come home on a particular weekend. If you wish to go home on that weekend, and you have been planning it together for some time, there is no problem. If, however, this is the first you have heard of this idea and you already have plans for that weekend, it is up to you to politely but firmly say so.

That is a good example of expectation based on past history. If through childhood and as an adult you have always submitted to your mother's requests, it is a pattern of behaviour which you must now consciously break. If submitting to your mother has been a long established routine, it will come as a surprise to her when you are no longer willing to do so. Importantly, this should be done without becoming angry. It is quite possible that your mother would become angry in this situation and you must avoid the danger of responding to anger with anger. Remember, you can disagree without being disagreeable. Whatever your temperament is, keep picturing yourself as being calm and rational. Keep remembering that as an adult you have the right to determine how you will spend your leisure time. In this frame of mind, you are more likely to remain focused and achieve your objectives.

Assertiveness is one of our characteristics which we can change if we wish to. The key is to remember that everyone, including ourselves, has rights. We have the right to think as we please. We have a right to choose our own course of action. We have the right to express our opinions. We have a right to make decisions.

As soon as we exercise our right to be assertive, we automatically take on the responsibility for the consequences of our actions. In doing so, we will get some things right and we will also make mistakes. As we mature from childhood into adulthood, taking responsibility is a part of life. We would not want to be people who make no decisions and take no responsibility. Being sufficiently assertive is a major facet of confidence, and confidence, as discussed earlier, is the cornerstone of happiness.

THE DESIRE TO BE ATTRACTIVE

We all have the desire to be attractive to other people. On reading the heading above, "the desire to be attractive," did you immediately think of physical attractiveness? If you did, you are not alone. Many people first think of attractiveness in purely physical terms. But physical beauty is only one part of human attractiveness and in the next section we will talk more about physical appearance. To start with, however, let us look at all the other characteristics which make people attractive to each other.

When we think about our attractiveness to others, we should not confine these thoughts to people whom we might consider as being potential romantic partners. In the course of our daily lives, we come across a whole range of people, both genders, all ages and from a variety of backgrounds. We can look for attractive features in all of them and we in turn can be attractive to them.

A psychologist, who normally only works with adults, became involved in a two-day programme testing playground games in a primary school. With very little experience of children, he now suddenly found himself surrounded by about 200 of them. What truly surprised him was how quickly some of these children stood out from the crowd. Some of them clearly exhibited far more energy and enthusiasm. Some of them had an uninhibited sense of sheer joy. For a lucky few, these qualities were combined with physical attractiveness. More importantly, however, there were many children who exuded openness and happiness who were not obviously physically attractive. These children were attractive because they had outstanding character and personality.

Beauty is in the eye of the beholder and we must be the first person to behold our own beauty and that of other people.

It is often said that the people we find most attractive are those who show an interest in us. If someone shows an interest in us, it means that we have passed their acceptability test. By that I mean that we all make instant judgments. We will quickly decide, in every encounter, whether or not we wish to engage further with that person.

The most interesting conversation we can hold usually involves talking about ourselves or those issues which particularly interest or affect us. So a good starting point to being attractive to others is to show an interest in them. The easiest way to do this is to be genuinely interested in everyone we meet. Whatever questions we ask of them will be based on sincere interest. This is very easy. After all, we enjoy reading stories and watching television programmes. These are really no more than studies in human character which are naturally of interest to all of us. The only difference is that in a book or film the characters are revealed to us. In real life, we have to actively seek out this information ourselves.

Sooner or later, when we have been asking about someone else, talking about their interests and seeking their opinions, they in turn will become curious about us and turn the conversation in our direction.

We all like to be with people who are interesting. Other people become interesting to us when they have something to say which is original, different or amusing. Think of someone you know who falls into this category. How did they develop these skills? No one is born with these qualities. We learn them in the same way that we learn any other skill. What we are able to talk about is the result of what we have seen, read and personally experienced.

We can certainly control what we watch on television and choose the material we read. If we confine ourselves to watching exactly the same television programs as our peers, we will certainly be able to discuss those. This can create a useful, comfortable bonding. It does not, however, make us unique in any way or more interesting. While I do not propose that we should seek to be contentious, solely for the purpose of grabbing attention, we can try to look at issues in a fresh way. When any of us discuss relationships, sports, social issues, politics or most other things, there is a tendency for our comments to be black and white. We come down heavily and inflexibly on one side of the argument. There is also a tendency for all of us to seek out people and information which confirms the beliefs we already hold.

As an example, I would cite the case of a friend who is violently opposed to American international policy. He absorbs any information which supports his beliefs without questioning the impartiality of validity of the source of criticism. Conversely, he will not even read anything that may in any way be contrary to his views. So the issue here is not whether American foreign policy is right or wrong. The issue is whether we are sufficiently open-minded to look at both sides of this or any other argument before forming and retaining our opinion.

With personal encounters, it would surely be more interesting to look at individual circumstances and comment on both the merits and deficiencies. That is not to say that we should not form strong opinions about issues which are important to us. It does suggest that we should be sufficiently open-minded to ask someone with differing opinions to elaborate on why they hold certain views or opinions.

If we have asked someone for their opinion, do we actually listen carefully to their answer? Or do we switch off and just wait for them to stop talking so that we can reiterate what we ourselves already think?

Listening is a skill and an art which all of us benefit from developing. Most people think that listening is totally passive, but it is not. If we are really listening to someone, we should be able to repeat back to them the full essence of what they have said and the meaning they were trying to convey. In any kind of important communication, such as an argument or negotiation, this is helpful to both sides. The more heated and irrational someone is, the more important it is to clarify what we think they are trying to say and to let them know this is our understanding of what they are saying.

If we engage openly with people, we will be showing them that we respect their opinions and their right to hold these opinions. They in turn may or may not respect our opinions and our right to hold these opinions. While we can certainly try to persuade, we cannot and will never be able to control other people in the way they think. We can, however, create an environment in which we all have room to manoeuvre, and hopefully one in which we can develop mutual respect.

Whether or not other people find us attractive depends to a very large extent on our own attitude. Are we open, positive and receptive? Does our speech and body language reflect this? Problems arise when we are solely interested in getting what we want. When there is no interest in or allowance for the needs and concerns of other people. The concept of a win-win situation applies just as much to conversations as to business deals.

A very successful businessman told me that, in every deal he creates, he leaves something on the table for the other person. By this he means that in negotiating a deal he does not seek to have all the benefit for himself and little or no benefit for the person with whom he is dealing. Quite the reverse. He wishes to ensure that in every deal he negotiates there is benefit for everyone involved. This business philosophy has done more than merely make him rich. He has the respect of all the people with whom he does business. Moreover, because he is known as a maker of fair deals, business people come to him when they have suitable opportunities.

Our daily lives are very similar to creating business deals. Our exchanges with other people involve some form of transaction. It may be as simple as greeting someone we know or helping a neighbour with a simple DIY job. Whatever the circumstances, it will work best if, over the long-term, there is both giving and taking. In other words, there is a win-win situation. While I have referred here to giving and taking, I do know from personal experience that the best way to make this work is by not keeping score. If we forget about who did what and when, we enter every encounter with the spirit of openness and generosity.

When people give something to us, even if it is as simple as making eye contact or smiling, we are instinctively pleased. We can easily give those small gifts to other people. Many of the best gifts are available for all of us to give. That is, they do not require money or anything material. The greatest gift we can give to anyone is to acknowledge them; to recognise their human qualities are every bit as important as our own.

Should we wish to do so, we can also go beyond this. We all like to receive compliments but there is also something rewarding about giving compliments and seeing the pleasure they create. This is not to suggest that compliments should be fabricated, insincere or in any way inappropriate. But if a compliment is warranted, we have the choice of either giving that compliment or withholding it. Sometimes it takes courage to give a compliment, but if done with complete sincerity it will be received in that way.

Recently I needed to have a service call for a washing machine which was no longer functioning. For various reasons, I had to contact the manufacturer directly to get a service call. I went through all the usual frustrations of phone menus and interminable waiting until a call centre operator finally spoke to me. The first thing they informed me about was an excessively high call out charge which had to be paid by credit card over the phone regardless of what the service man would eventually find. I was also told that any parts would be charged as extra and I knew that these would be expensive.

When the service man finally did arrive a week later, it was his last appointment of the day. Despite being a little late and tired, he took his time stripping down the machine and looking carefully for the cause of the problem. He replaced a relatively inexpensive part which solved the problem. He then went on to spend a considerable amount of time instructing me how to use the machine to its best advantage; how to get the best results, with the minimum energy usage; and how to ensure that I did not cause a similar problem again.

I felt that this service man had done a first-rate job. I thanked him for the effort he had gone to in explaining what had gone wrong and why. I told him that I felt I was lucky to have had such a knowledgeable and conscientious service call.

This was not a question of trying to be clever and it had no bearing on the final cost of the service call. I just felt that this man had done a really good job and there was no reason why I should not tell him that. We usually hear from people quickly enough when they are not satisfied. Perhaps we should all be as ready to show our gratitude when we are satisfied.

We have the ability to be positive in our dealings with other people. Our voice, our physical stance and what we say can set the tone for most encounters. This is particularly interesting because it means that we can and do influence the way in which other people react to us. If we anticipate that people will be courteous to us, they probably will be. If we anticipate that people will be rude to us, they probably will be. Our own attitudes and expectations often play a part in creating the outcome of any situation.

Our attractiveness to other people does depend on what we have to offer and the opinion we have of ourselves. The good news is that we can all develop a whole range of skills which will make us attractive to many people. No-one is attractive to absolutely everyone else and we should not try to be. As time goes by, we can however broaden our appeal if that is what we wish to do. We can work on and develop our social skills in the same way that we learn and develop our ability in any other craft. We can learn the art of allowing other people to find us attractive.

PHYSICAL ATTRACTIVENESS

Jean Cocteau said: *"The privileges of beauty are enormous."* In my opinion, he was only partly correct. When we think of someone who is physically attractive, we are in reality saying that we would like to have sex with them or that we fully understand why other people would wish to have sex with them. That is pure hormonal sex, which takes absolutely no account of what the person is like, what motivates them and whether or not we like them as a human being. Television news readers are often chosen because they have what the media industry refers to as the "fanciability factor."

Even this is subjective and cultural. There is a huge difference between the type of person you will see reading the news on the BBC and the identikit news readers to be found on American television. Broadly speaking, female newsreaders in the UK will be of the "gentle feminine" variety, whereas their counterparts in the USA will all have implausibly perfect teeth and be much more forthright.

There are people of both genders who have the mixed blessing of being physically attractive. If people are primarily interested in you because they want to have sex with you, the net result is that you are little more than a sex object. I have met people who have been gifted with extraordinarily good looks. In some cases, this has allowed them to become socially lazy. By this I mean that they have never made the effort to truly develop their personality. Sexually, some very attractive (or very rich) people never bother to learn how to give pleasure to their partner. Simply being in demand as a sexual partner and then bestowing their gifts is the only reward they feel they are required to offer.

Strangely enough, there is also a paradox which applies to very good looking people. Because they are so good looking, people of average looks sometimes mistakenly think that the good looking person does not need their company and would not be interested in them and so they do not approach. The net result is that the exceptionally good looking can sometimes be isolated by their good looks.

For some young people, their major goal in life is the ability to have as much sex as they want and pretty well with whomever they want. It would be foolish to deny the power of our hormones, but the greatest satisfaction and rewards in life come from the intimacy we feel with people whom we genuinely care about. My advice to good looking people is to be grateful for the gifts that nature has bestowed on them and to see these as a wonderful foundation on which to build.

Remember also that as age takes its toll and the good looks fade, these people are left without the personality resources to engage the attention of others. A very famous movie star was interviewed on a recent television chat show. This actor's wonderful good looks and amazing physique had captured the hearts of millions of women and the envy of millions of men. In the interview, this man came across as inarticulate and rather boring. You could still see faded signs of the original good looks, but without a script he had nothing of interest to say.

Compare this with other performers who may not have been as physically attractive. When we see them interviewed on chat shows they seem to have an endless repertoire of anecdotes and funny stories. These people are relying on a different set of gifts. They are using their full range of skills as an entertainer. They give the gift of entertainment rather than just being a passive object of beauty.

Good looks alone are a poor substitute for a fully rounded character. It is like the pyrrhic victory of being born with inherited wealth. It is nice and comforting but usually does not produce the satisfaction which follows the motivation and drive found in those less favoured with attractive looks or wealth. In the case of physical beauty, we know that this asset will decline year by year until the day they die. Beauty can leave someone mentally and emotionally undeveloped. What we should all seek to develop is a combination of qualities which make us attractive, and yes, physical attractiveness is a part of this package.

If we are not obviously physically attractive, does it matter? That is a question which only the individual can answer. If the desire to be attractive to other people is strong enough, we all have the ability to be attractive. This does not mean that we can magically create some situation in which heads will turn every time we walk past. What it does mean is that we all have the opportunity to enhance facets of ourselves which other people find attractive. We started off by talking about physical attractiveness and to some extent there is something which all of us can do about this. Through keeping in shape and by dressing appropriately, we can be more physically attractive. If we take plenty of exercise, we will feel fit. When we feel fit, we project a sense of health and well-being which in itself is an attractive feature.

How we present ourselves is also a factor in our physical attractiveness. Whatever our body shape or appearance, we can enhance it or detract from it by our choice of clothes and hairstyle. Blindly following the style that is in vogue has the potential to be disastrous. Certain styles suit certain people but not others. One example was the trend for young women to have a bare midriff. This style possibly suits the slim but does not flatter the overweight. So someone who is a little overweight would be better not to adopt this style rather than risk being referred to in derogatory terms such as "muffin top"

Having said that, there is the story of a mini-skirted teenage girl, who in the 1960s, was told by her mother that she looked awful. "But" replied the girl, "I feel wonderful." If we feel wonderful about ourselves, that alone is a great gift.

Our weight, and the ability to control it, is an emotive subject.

Referring to the elegance and style of Parisian women, an American fashion editor recently said that the main difference between an American woman and a French woman is about ten kilos.

Judgment is one of the most important skills we can develop. Interestingly, the part of the brain responsible for judgment is one of the last to develop. It is not fully formed and functioning until we are over 20. It is not surprising therefore, that teenagers consistently make errors of judgment. It is important that in later life we understand the enormous influence that our judgment has on our lives and to hone our judging skills.

Working on our physical appearance is not a contradiction to what has been said earlier. It is simply a matter of getting things in the correct balance. We all have strengths and weaknesses. Our aim is sometimes to make our own package of qualities attractive to other people. Some people may object to this, arguing that we are who we are, that others can either accept us or reject us, and the last thing we should do is try to pander to what others consider to be acceptable or desirable.

The response to that relates to what we ourselves want. If we are happy with the situation in which we find ourselves that is fine. If we want things to be different, we must use sound judgment and do something to make them different. Remember again the saying, *"If you always do what you have always done you will always get what you have always got"*.

Coco Chanel said that if a woman dresses shabbily, people will notice the dress. If she dresses impeccably, they will notice the woman.

On the subject of physical beauty, I recently saw some pictures of a gawky and not particularly attractive girl called Norma Jeane Baker. No one who has seen these pictures would describe the young girl as being physically attractive or even cute. That same girl went on to use masses of make-up and to dress in the most provocative way she could which is how Norma Jeane metamorphosed into Marilyn Monroe. She went on to become one of the greatest sex symbols and an icon of feminine desirability. She is not alone. Many people become more attractive as they mature, and sometimes fashion swings move them into the frame of currently perceived beauty.

BEING POSITIVE, PEACEFUL AND ACCEPTING

John Milton wrote: "*The mind is its own place and in itself can make a heaven of hell and a hell of heaven.*"

All of us have had the experience of being with someone who is upbeat, cheerful and enthusiastic. On parting we feel uplifted, buoyant and happy to be alive. We probably also feel that we have been seen, heard and included. Conversely, we all know people whose conversation is one long stream of inward looking complaints and negativity. A session with them leaves us feeling miserable and depressed. So what type of person are you? What type of person would you like to be? You can choose to lift other people's spirits and your own or you can choose to be boring and depressive.

As I have said before, there is a tendency for us to live within our own expectations. If we think that the world is without hope, we will see everything in that light. If we seek out that which is good, we will find it. This in no way suggests that we should adopt a purely Pollyanna attitude to life. There are, of course, problems in the world, and there are problems and difficulties within our own lives. Positive thinking teaches us to recognise the problems and react to them appropriately, while at the same time focusing on that which is good and beneficial. If we seek out and focus on the most positive outcome in any situation that will create the best environment in which it can be achieved.

We all have a sense of the circumstances which would for us be ideal, but usually this is different to reality. Sadly, reality is rarely idyllic and that is why in paintings we tend to idealise events, such as the Christmas nativity scene, which is an early example of editing out the harshness of reality.

Our disposition towards life is usually learnt in our homes during childhood. If the people around us are constantly being negative or positive, we will adopt that attitude. Peer pressure in school or the workplace is also strongly influential. Say, for example, someone is surrounded by colleagues who live on a diet of cynicism. It would not, therefore, be surprising if he too has become cynical. Should he wish to do so however, he has the choice of seeing things in a more positive way. Surely if he had the courage to do so, he would become a breath of fresh air within the otherwise stultifying world of the cynics?

There is the story of a girl who e-mailed her parents from a very expensive boarding school where she was studying. She told them that she had become pregnant and was going to run away with her biker boyfriend. Her distraught mother rushed to the school. When she questioned her daughter, she found the girl was not pregnant, did not have a biker boyfriend and had no intention of running away. "But," her daughter said, "I have failed most of my exams and just wanted to make sure that you saw this in perspective".

The fact is that failing exams is certainly not what any parent or student wants. On the other hand, we know what the answer would be if we said to a parent whose child had a serious illness. Which would you prefer? That your child has a terminal illness or that they were healthy but failed all their exams? The counter argument to this is that simply because the situation could be worse does not make it acceptable or desirable.

A man in his late twenties was caught by the police driving in excess of 130 miles per hour. Rightly he was charged and convicted for this offence. He was fined, lost his driving licence for a period of time and suffered long-term effects such as increased difficulty in obtaining insurance and its higher cost.

His parents felt a range of emotions which included anger at the fact that he had been so irresponsible. They were upset that he lost his licence and understood that there would be long-term effects of this action. At the same time, they took comfort from the fact that the incident had not been different. They were well aware that they could have received a phone call in the middle of the night telling them that their son had been badly injured or killed in a high-speed accident. As worrying was the thought that their son could have been responsible for an accident which caused serious injury or took the life of someone else. They also hoped that being stopped by the police and the subsequent court appearance would provide a useful lesson.

As for the driver, did it teach him a lesson? His reaction to the whole affair was that he was a first-rate driver who was not posing a threat to himself or anyone else. He just had the misfortune to pass an unmarked police car. Seeing beyond his own desire to drive fast to the potential consequences was something that he just did not have the sense and maturity to understand. The point here is that the same incident can be viewed in different ways. One sees only the negative while the other takes a balanced view and is grateful for the positive aspects.

Thinking about death and serious injury is highly appropriate in the context of positive thinking. If the opposite of positive thinking is negative thinking and worry, it is logical to conclude that the most worrying things that could happen to us are death or serious physical impairment. We still however manage to worry about many things which in reality are completely insignificant. I remember worrying about the fact that a warning light had come up on the dashboard of my car. Rather than thinking about all of the potential consequences of an engine problem and the cost that would involve, I should have thought how wonderful technology is and that I did get a warning in advance of a potentially serious problem.

It turned out that the warning light had come on as a result of unusually damp weather conditions. As soon as the weather brightened up, the warning light went out. Looking back on this incident, I am aware of the fact that I used up emotional energy completely unnecessarily. That is not to say that we should ignore warning signals whether they are real or metaphorical. It does mean that many of us worry about things unduly. It does mean that, rather than worry, we should think about the issue, then plan and finally act appropriately.

Some of us are more prone to worry than others. It is as if each of us has a worry quota which we will fill regardless of how serious the events in our lives actually are. It has also been said that "worry is the interest you pay on a debt you may not owe".

Maya Angelou said, *"You can tell a lot about a person by the way they handle these three things: a rainy day, lost luggage and tangled Christmas tree lights."*

Wendell Berry found his own solution and wrote most beautifully, *"When despair for the world grows in me and I wake in the night at the least sound, in fear of what my life and my children's life may be, I go and lie down where the wood drake rests in his beauty on the water and the great heron feeds. I come into the peace of wild things who do not tax their lives with forethought of grief. I come into the presence of still water. And I feel above me that the day-blind stars waiting for their light. For a time I rest in the grace of the world and am free."*

Both worry and positive thinking have a direct physical effect on our bodies. These emotions cause us to release hormones into the bloodstream. The word hormone comes from the Greek meaning to "arouse activity." When we are nervous and frightened our bodies produce cortisol. Throughout the ages, this has been useful to us in the "fight or flight" response but is very harmful in our modern sedentary lives. Cortisol is produced by the adrenal glands and it is important for normal health. It allows the body to quickly produce a high level of energy. If, however, this energy is not burnt off through physical activity, it can leave us with increased blood pressure, blood sugar imbalances and sometimes with impaired cognitive performance. It is important that we keep our worry and fear emotions under control so that in turn we do not create the potential for long-term damage to our bodies.

At the other end of the scale, when we think about what we enjoy most, our bodies release endorphins which are a form of morphine naturally produced within the body. Endorphins are not only analgesics and painkillers but they also give a pervasive sense of well-being and happiness. Athletes such as marathon runners often say that at a certain stage of their exercise, they start to feel mildly euphoric. Something they call the "runner's high." This is because the body is under stress and starts to release endorphins in order to neutralise the pain of endurance running, which then allows the body to continue working as if it were in a genuine fight or flight situation.

William Bloom, author of the book "The Endorphin Effect", tells the story that for many years he studied and practised the art of meditation. His search for enlightenment took him to exotic places like India and the parched deserts of Morocco. Years later when he was leading a meditation group in England, he asked the participants about the circumstances in their lives which produced the greatest sense of happiness and well-being. He was surprised when one woman said that for her the greatest sense of calm came when she was sitting in a comfortable armchair, rhythmically stroking her cat.

We do not have to travel to the far corners of the earth to find peace. We have to feed and nurture ourselves mentally and physically. It is only when we have good emotional balance and energy that we in turn can give these gifts to other people. In order for us to be generous, show gratitude and be able to support and love others, we ourselves must feel we are endowed with these gifts.

PERSONALITY, ATTRACTIVENESS AND HUMOUR

The very first essay written by a student at university had the engaging title "The Epithets of the Greek Gods." When his tutor called him in to discuss this he expected the tutor to say how well he had done. In fact, looking down at the paper, the tutor started off in a slow voice with the comment, *"I suppose it was alright."* *"But,"* he went on….. *"it was so boring."*

The student was shocked and hurt. How could the tutor think his masterpiece was boring? Looking back, he knows that the tutor gave him some of the most useful feedback he ever received. In two short sentences the tutor taught the valuable lesson that simply being factually correct is not enough. All human beings are drawn to things which catch our interest.

We all like to be entertained and amused. At school, my favourite subject was history because history presented properly is just like storytelling. At university, I really looked forward to my English literature classes. This again is because literature is full of emotion and the unexpected. Moreover, the people who taught these courses could be relied upon to be thought provoking and to make us laugh.

Sadly, educational institutions do not teach us the really important things in life, such as for men, how to undo a bra strap smoothly and quickly with one hand, or how to be humorous. Humour surprises. It does not have to say anything earth shatteringly clever but sometimes uses incongruity or leads us away from what commonsense would expect. There is an inscription over a bar frequented by medical students which makes many people laugh. It reads, "I'd rather have a full bottle in front of me than a full frontal lobotomy" The would-be politician, the late "Lord" Sutch, asked the rhetorical question "Why is there only one Monopolies Commission?" He could also have asked if there was another word for thesaurus.

The fact is, we gravitate towards people who entertain us and make us laugh. They may be dealing with serious subjects such as politics or science but if they are able to wrap their message in humour we are more likely to listen to them. One politician looked dismayed after an election in which he lost an apparently safe seat. He said he had shaken hands with 40% of his constituents. But, he noted laconically, he must also have shaken the confidence of the other 60%.

GSOH — the abbreviation for "good sense of humour." Anyone who has ever been involved in Internet or newspaper dating will be very familiar with this acronym. Having a good sense of humour, or requiring one in a potential partner, is high on the list of qualities which all of us seek. We all love to laugh. If we have the ability to make other people laugh, they will always seek out our company.

This does not mean that we should all try to become stand-up comedians. A constant stream of gags can be strained and quite tiring. As listeners, we do not want to feel that we are required to laugh. Most of our lives revolve around relatively serious issues such as the work we do. Humour is most valuable when it is spontaneous, original and relevant to the situation.

On his first day of National Service, a rather gentle Cambridge graduate was being browbeaten by an aggressive sergeant major who thrust his heavy pace stick into the recruit's chest and then said "There's a nasty piece of shit at the end of this stick." To which the graduate immediately replied, "Not at this end."

There are risks involved in trying to be funny. We have all said something which was meant to be funny but which fell completely flat. Just as we would all like to be thought of as witty and amusing, we are all afraid of being thought of as a perennial teller of bad jokes and un-amusing anecdotes. So it is easier for all of us to avoid trying to be funny or amusing. Although this is the safe option, it does take from us the opportunity to give someone else the gift of laughter. It takes from us the opportunity for other people to see our lighter side and to find us amusing and interesting.

Wayne Gretzky, the great Canadian ice hockey player, said, "*You will always miss 100% of the shots you do not take.*" We will all miss 100% of the humour we do not attempt.

A few years ago I met a woman who told me that, as a result of shyness she had not made a speech at her 50th birthday party and that she had regretted it. I told her that I had made a speech at my 50th birthday party – but that everyone else had regretted it.

After writing the somewhat obscure play, "Rosencrantz and Guildenstern are Dead," the author Tom Stoppard was asked what it was about. His reply was, "*It's about to make me very rich.*" Similarly, when Charles Saatchi first started to exhibit modern art from communist China he was asked how free the Chinese were. "*Free!*", he exclaimed. "*You should see the prices they charge*".

There is a lovely story about an elderly woman who received a parking ticket because her "disabled" permit had become bleached by the sun on the dashboard of her car and was now unreadable. The young council official who cancelled her parking ticket and issued her with a new disabled badge suggested that she should now "put it where the sun don't shine."

Wit is verbal playfulness, whereas jokes are set pieces based on situation or character. That is not to say that there is no place for this type of humour. If something amused us in the past there is no reason why that humour cannot be reused in the future. On leaving a party, Groucho Marx once famously said to his host, "*I've had a great evening. But this was not it.*" We can use this humour in a parallel form. For example, on leaving a sporting event, we could say that we have seen our team play really well. But not today!

Somerset Maugham said, "*The ability to quote is a serviceable substitute for wit.*"

Humour releases tension. In set piece humour, the joke sets up the tension which is then released in an unexpected way. The comedian Tommy Cooper said, "*The other week I had to share my dressing room with a monkey. The producer came in and said, I'm sorry about this. That's OK, I replied. He said I wasn't talking to you.*"

The Daily Telegraph ran an obituary for Melita Norwood. It described her as a jam-making great grandmother who, in 1999, was found to have been spying on behalf of the Russians for over four decades. They then went on to use some verbal playfulness to make this situation humorous. The newspaper described Mrs Norwood as "*the Bolshevik of Bexley Heath. The spy who came in from the Co-op.*"

Similar light-heartedness was applied to a serious subject when it was said that Jock Delves Broughton shot Lord Erroll in the head. He later shot himself in the Adelphi hotel. Concerning the same people, Frances Osborne wrote, "*Joss (Lord Erroll) fell in love with another man's house – and stole his wife in order to get it.*"

Sometimes humour is merely a way of defusing the consequences of telling the truth. In a meeting with an overseas dignitary, the Foreign Secretary, Lord Carrington is said to have passed a note to the Prime Minister, Margaret Thatcher. The note read, "*The poor chap has come 600 miles. Do let him say something.*"

On other occasions, the tension which already exists can through the use of humour be dissipated. People in genuinely hazardous and dangerous situations frequently use humour to give a brief respite from the stress. Hospitals, police stations and the fire service are all well-known examples of this. Armed forces personnel in battle situations use black humour not only to relieve stress but also to bond with their fellow soldiers. Through humour combined with imminent danger, soldiers throughout the ages have felt the wonderful camaraderie expressed by Shakespeare in Henry V with the moving sentiment, "*We few... we happy few... we band of brothers.*"

Humour is a great medium for connecting. If we laugh at the same things, we share a similar sense of humour. If we find the same things funny, we then have something in common. If we have something in common, we are part of a group. Surely all of us have at some time laughed at a joke which we did not even understand. We do this because it shows we are part of the group. We also laugh when we are part of a group because laughter is infectious. If everyone around us is laughing, it is very hard for us to remain sombre. We all understand that when people laugh with us they are likely to be receptive to the message we wish to give. Salespeople use humour, and one famous actress said happily of her favourite suitor that he simply laughed her into bed.

Humour can be used to sugar coat even the most bitter tasting pill. It is widely thought in the legal profession that if a defence barrister can make the jury laugh, they are more likely to acquit. Although sometimes the defendant manages to create laughter on his own. When trying to engender sympathy for his client as the product of a disturbed childhood, a barrister asked the accused why he robbed banks. The simple answer the robber gave was, "*Because that's where the money is.*"

Roedean is a prestigious girls school located on the South Downs overlooking the sea near Brighton. Its austere, fortress-like buildings led to the nickname, "Colditz on the cliffs." During the war, the girls were evacuated and servicemen were billeted in this Victorian facility. A source of amusement for many of them was the ancient bell system found throughout the school, for some bells were labelled, "*Ring if you require a mistress.*"

Laughter releases endorphins into our bloodstream. So when we laugh (or even if we are just thinking warm, comfortable thoughts), we get the uplifting and beneficial effects of the endorphins.

Using humour takes courage. When we say something which

is intended to be funny, we are revealing something about our own personality. Our humour may reveal that we like or dislike subjects as diverse as poetry or blood sports. Just as humour can form bonds, it can also alienate. If our listener does not find humour in the same things that we find funny, they may well decide that we are not the type of person with whom they wish to socialise.

Occupational jokes can be both bonding and separating. For example, doctors using medical terminology may well say things which are humorous only to another medical practitioner. While these jokes create a bond with other medical staff, they also cause separation with non-medical people. Conversely, no special terminology needs to be known to understand what was said in an after-dinner speech by a diplomat who asked the question, *"What is the difference between a diplomat and a camel?"* To which the reply was, *"A camel can work for three weeks without having a drink and a diplomat can drink for three weeks without doing any work."*

There is the old saying that many a true word is spoken in jest. Gerald Ratner had built up a successful chain of jewellery shops. There were several stores in London and many more were to be found on the high streets of major British towns. At an important business conference, Ratner cracked a joke. He said that in his shops they sold a decanter and four glasses for £9.95. How could they do this so cheaply? Because the product was crap! This joke produced enormous laughter, which is what Ratner wanted. But this joke also cost him his business because the following day there were newspaper headlines saying that the owner of Ratners openly admitted to the shoddy quality of their products. Suddenly Ratners was no longer an acceptable, let alone desirable, store from which to buy an engagement ring or any other cherished presents.

Humour is funny because it quickly leads us in a direction which we were not expecting. P. J. O'Rourke said that there are a number of mechanical devices which increase sexual arousal, particularly in women, and chief among these is the Mercedes-Benz 380SL convertible.

One man who visited his aged mother, who was in the early stages of dementia, was aware of how dated her television set was and asked her if she would like a new one. Her reply was that she would like a new set because she didn't like the programmes on this one.

Sex is a common theme used in humour. There is absolutely no reason why sex should not be used as a vehicle for humour, but because people's attitude to sex varies so much, it is a subject which can cause offence, even when no offence is intended. Kathy Lette joked that May West had so many men in her life that she kept a "bonk" account. The humour here is by a woman about a woman. It is in no way offensive and the humour is derived solely from a pun.

Contrast this with an after-dinner speech given by a female judge at a police dinner. Rightly or wrongly, she was apparently under the impression that the predominantly male police force liked bawdy humour. Perhaps with the intention of not wishing to appear aloof, she peppered her speech with a number of crude jokes. This was, however, an error of judgment. What she had not taken into account was the fact that most of these men were accompanied by their wives. The psychology of that evening was such that the men were looking forward to a polished speech by a judge. They wanted and expected to bask in the reflection of her class and prestige, not to be patronised.

People giving formal speeches sometimes inject a little humour by making deliberate or unintentional mistakes. One doctor who was assumed to be talking about "motor neurone disease" referred to it as "neuter moron disease." Another speaker who was referring to a miniscule bug which was devastating forests meant to say, "the pinewood nematode is a microscopic organism." What he actually referred to was "a microscopic orgasm."

It is a cultural stereotype and misconception to think that the

Germans do not have a sense of humour. During the war the British tried to deceive the Germans by building "mock" facilities which would draw their bombers away from real targets. When the Germans spotted one of these fake "harbour facilities" built out of plywood they responded by dropping a wooden bomb on it.

When humour goes wrong it can be painful for both the speaker and for the listener. For this reason, many people are scared to use humour. It is this fear of using humour which turns us into passive absorbers of humour rather than generators of laughter. The solution to this is to start developing our ability to use humour in the same way that we develop any other skill. If we want to learn to climb, we do not start on Everest. We start off by getting fit and doing some hill walking before progressing to steeper climbs.

Being humorous is a skill we learn. A common misconception is that some people are born funny and some people are not. People who have learnt to be humorous have done so through consciously or subconsciously observing what makes people laugh. They have then had the courage to try using humour in the form of existing jokes they have heard before, or by following the verbal or physical patterns which people find amusing.

There are literally hundreds of books which are humorous. There are books about humour and even books which simply contain a never-ending variety of jokes. We can watch films and TV programmes which use verbal humour and which we find funny. In so doing, we can develop our minds to find the humorous connection. Not everything we read, hear or see will be funny. For me, it is like panning for gold. I am constantly looking out for the nugget of real humour. We can develop our ability to be humorous in exactly the same way that a footballer develops his ability. That is by concentrating on the subject, practising it and in turn forming the neural pathways which allow us to see appropriate humour quickly.

Then through practice we develop the courage to say things

which we think are funny. If we genuinely think something is amusing and it makes us laugh, there is a high probability that it will make other people, with similar values, laugh as well. Like any skill we wish to acquire, the ability to use humour is developed slowly but will never be developed if we do not consciously work to develop it.

The ability to develop and use good judgment is important in every facet of our lives. This includes our ability to judge how to use humour appropriately and effectively. Cultural backgrounds have a strong influence on our sense of humour. Moreover, if someone makes racist or sexist remarks under the guise of humour, we may well decide that they are not the type of person with whom we wish to socialise.

Keep focusing on the prize of humour. The prize is that we will laugh more and that the people around us will laugh more. The prize is that we will be able to contribute more in social situations and that people will enjoy our company and include us more frequently for that reason.

We are more than mere mind and body. We humans wish to consider our spiritual dimension and that is what we shall do in the next level.

LEVEL 5 - COGNITIVE NEEDS

Knowledge, meaning, self-awareness, religious & spiritual choice

RITUAL AND TRADITION

The Canadian prairies stretch for two thousand miles between Ontario and the Rocky Mountains. The land is flat, boring and featureless other than the numerous, and equally featureless, small bodies of water called sloughs. So I was genuinely surprised when a young man from rural Saskatchewan told me how amazingly beautiful his home town was. My first reaction was that, because he had never travelled anywhere else, he did not know what real beauty looked like.

Later, when I was living on the prairies and heavily involved in photography, I set up a small business selling large size original photographic prints. My portfolio included atmospheric pictures of mediaeval European cities and exotic pictures from South-east Asia. These however did not sell. What did sell were pictures of snow swept prairies, long abandoned homesteads and migratory ducks flying low over swampy grasslands. These scenes sold because the people buying them could all identify with the pictures.

We all have a past which is irrevocably linked with elements of who we think we are. Even people whose lives have taken them on an incredible trajectory of success and affluence feel nostalgia for the place of their childhood. It is often with disappointment that we find some of the fixtures of our youth have been changed. Old buildings demolished and urban sprawl covering what we remember as having been open countryside.

Deep down most of us are afraid of change. The new is unknown and therefore frightening. We need a sense of belonging which is achieved through a recognisable stream of consistency.

We want to feel that however much things do change, we are connected by an ongoing continuity, which has run through past generations and now holds us in its framework. We embrace the comfort given to us by ritual and tradition through acknowledging the changing climatic seasons and celebrating human ones.

Whether we are religious or not, much of our ritual and tradition is tied to religious festivals. Celebrating Christmas is obviously a Christian festival and yet for many people the significance lies more in the fact that their family is brought together. Similarly, the American festival of Thanksgiving, which takes place on the fourth Thursday in November, is even more significant for the very reason that it is a secular event. It is a time when all religions and faiths can unite in celebration. Even if it does not happen at any other time of year, many people know they will be reuniting on December 25th or for Thanksgiving.

We are all of us, to a greater or lesser extent, ritualistic and habitual. We all make our cup of tea in a certain way and most of us pragmatically keep our car keys in the same place. The more important rituals such as weddings and funerals acknowledge significant change and give us a recognised format in which to witness and legitimise them. They provide a steadying hand-hold on our otherwise shaky and uncertain path through life.

FAITH

We have a need for faith because of the brevity of life and existential uncertainty.

St. Bede first recorded the allegorical story of a sparrow flying through the great hall of a Saxon nobleman's house. On a harsh winter's day the sparrow entered by one door, briefly passed through the warmth, comfort and security of the hall before departing through the door at the other end, returning once more to the cold and dangerous unknown.

Faith is belief and trust. It comes at different times, in different situations and in varying degrees of strength. Faith is essential to all our lives. If we believed and trusted in nothing, we would live in a permanent state of fear and uncertainty. At its most basic level, we must have faith that when we turn on a tap water will flow out. We have faith in the belief that our car will start on most mornings. As we get to know people, we decide how much faith to grant them. How much trust we have in them. We make the transition from having no knowledge about them to holding the belief that they will act in a certain way.

Our faith in everyday life is based on experience. If we see the same cause and effect over and over again, we have trust that the sequence will continue. Beyond logic, we have such a strong desire to "remain in the warmth and security of this hall," or the desire to find an even better one, that we willingly accept faith without the usual pre-requisite of experience.

Psalm 23 shows both our yearning for security and our willingness to have faith.

"Goodness and mercy all my life,
Shall surely follow me:
And in God's house for evermore,
My dwelling place shall be"

Some people would say that developing or finding faith without sophistry and prejudice is the highest state we can achieve.

RELIGIOUS CHOICE

Once we have opened a bank account very few of us can be bothered to close it down and start an account at a different bank. On a far more important matter, it is known statistically very few people change religion. The vast majority of people follow the religion of the family and society into which they were born. Sometimes people vary the intensity of their religious practice and they may even make changes within their religious practice, such as moving from Protestantism to Catholicism. When asked to nominate their religion on official forms, the vast majority of people will write down the religion of their childhood. This would indicate that the vast majority of people simply accept the religion of their parents. The only choice they then make is how to interpret that religion and how much or how little faith they have in it.

There is no doubt that many people believe in a God and have faith in that God. The major religions of the world are all comparatively young. A belief in an omniscient supernatural power and man's ability to prevail upon it, together with the requirement to live by its rules, dates back to earliest man. Primitive societies lived with constant danger and uncertainty. Their survival was so precarious, and their understanding of the world so limited, that they took solace in the belief that through the understanding and appeasement of the forces around them, they could exert some control.

Earliest bipedal man, homo sapiens, evolved approximately 200,000 years ago; a mere blinking of the eye in geological terms. The hunter-gatherers of 50,000 years ago lived in small, nomadic, family units. One estimate has suggested that the entire human population in what is now East Africa could have been as small as 10,000 at that time. Descartes said that only humans think, and by inference, only humans have self-awareness. While this is not entirely true, the price we humans pay for self-awareness is an understanding and fear of our own mortality.

Furthermore, the ability to develop speech undoubtedly led not only to man's ability to communicate but also produced the capacity to think in a far more sophisticated way than the rest of the animal world. So it is the development of the human brain and thought processes which have allowed understanding, conceptualisation and belief. It is these concepts which differentiate and elevate man from other animals. It is also these concepts which lead many people to believe they are not merely the most successful animal on earth but a semi-divine one specially created by God and in God's image.

Daylight and warmth obviously came from the sun. The moon also appeared to have its own light and was clearly far more prominent than anything else in the night sky. Its regular but constantly changing shape gave it a sense of life and power. No wonder that human beings in all ages and in all cultures have wanted to worship and placate these father and mother "gods."

The interesting thing is that all these people were absolutely right to believe that we owe our very existence to the sun and the moon. The sun gives us heat, light and photosynthesis while the moon's gravitational force gives us tides and much of our weather systems, including that most valuable commodity, rain.

The only error was to believe that they could in any way influence these powers. The words of "Rule Britannia" are incorrect; it is not Britannia who rules the waves, but the moon.

As religious practice developed, it incorporated rules and guidelines for behaviour which included those actions which should be carried out and those which were prohibited. Many of these were practical issues which were absorbed into and combined with religious belief. For example, circumcision no doubt started simply as a practical way of maintaining hygiene. The avoidance of eating pork in a hot climate is a very practical way to avoid sickness. Many other taboos also evolved as a way of avoiding evils which manifested themselves as sickness.

The earliest "religions" all revolved around animism – the belief that everything in the world has an "animus" or spirit. Many people still believe that any living object, whether it is animal or plant, has a spirit which makes it unique in itself and also connects it with all other living things. A belief in animism can be held independently or incorporated into what we now consider to be the major religions of the world.

Hinduism, which is the oldest of the world's great religions, includes elements of animism. Unlike the other great religions, it was not founded by a single charismatic leader at a specific time. It has a variety of origins dating back approximately 4,000 years which have trickled down and combined, like the Himalayan mountain streams that feed the Ganges, to form the mighty river of Hinduism.

"Contrary to popular understanding, Hindus recognise one God – Brahman, the eternal origin who is the cause and foundation of all existence. The gods of the Hindu faith represent different expressions of Brahman. Different Hindu communities may have their own divinities whom they worship, but these are simply different ways of approaching the Ultimate.

Hindus recognise the three principal gods (and a pantheon of about 3,600 lesser gods):

Brahma, who created the universe.
Vishnu, who preserves the universe.
Shiva who destroys the universe.

Brahma is the Creator. However, Brahma is not worshipped in the same way as other gods because it is believed that his work

– that of creation – has been done. Vishnu, Shiva and other Vedic gods as well as their various representations are worshipped."[2]

Hinduism maintains the belief that the soul repeatedly reincarnates into different bodies until it reaches perfection and no longer needs to continue the cycle.

Judaism started as the religion of the Israelites some 3,500 years ago. It was Abraham who imposed his authority by renouncing the worship of numerous gods and establishing a monotheistic religion. Judaism was originally the religion of a single ethnic group. Today Jews, including those who are non-religious, identify themselves through their ethnic background. Others who are non-ethnic Jews become Jewish by conversion to Judaism.

Those who follow Judaism believe in a God who is ever present. A God who is involved in every aspect of their lives. A God who is strict but fair. A God who has no body and is therefore neither male nor female. A God who will be revealed in time and in whose presence they wish to be after death.

As a prescription for the way in which life is to be led, Judaism follows the Torah, which is also the first five books of the Bible. Judaism also has the Talmud, which is the oral history of the Jews which was written down in approximately 70 AD. The discovery of the Dead Sea Scrolls (between 1947 -1956) is of huge importance to Judaism because these are the earliest known documents written in Hebrew.

The next great religion is Buddhism. Or is Buddhism actually a religion? Perhaps it is more a philosophy for life. For Buddhists, the concept of God is really an abstract principle of goodness; therefore everyone creates their own God.

Approximately 2,500 years ago, Siddhartha Gautama was born in the town of Lumbini in present day Nepal. He was the

2. Copied directly from the Hinduism section of "Religion and Ethics", www.bbc.co.uk

son of the ruler and was brought up not only in luxury but also in isolation in order to prevent him from seeing any worldly unpleasantness. On his 29th birthday he secretly left the confines of his palace to learn about the world. He saw that old age brought physical deterioration. He saw that there was much illness and unhappiness in the world and he saw that death was inevitable.

Siddhartha conscientiously practised the accepted Hindu spiritual life as he understood it. Meditation, fasting and yogic practices designed to curb physical needs and desires. He felt that it was the never-ending wish of human beings to have what they cannot have, which leads to unhappiness. On coming to this conclusion or concept and laying down guidelines for life, he became known as the Buddha which means the "enlightened one."

Buddhists reject all forms of attachment, believing that they are the root cause of unhappiness. If we continue to want what is lost and gone, we can never be truly happy. In the practice of martial arts, some Buddhists burn off bodily energy while at the same time retaining a quiet and peaceful mind. To learn Zen, you have to be at one with nature – to flow as water flows. The message that Zen gives us is that it is up to each of us to find our own happiness.

The poet Wordsworth espoused a philosophy which would have been acceptable to Buddhists. He said that we are all part of nature and therefore all a part of God.

Some, but not all, present-day Buddhists still believe in the concept of reincarnation. A concept in which they carry forward their essence into another life, possibly that of an animal or another human being. Their essence is the subtlety of their mind devoid of specific information such as language and facts.

It is only when the perfect life has been achieved that an individual is able to step off the treadmill of reincarnation, having reached the state of Nirvana which is considered to be a state of liberation – of perfect peace.

Judaism did and still does believe that a messiah, a leader of the Jews, will be found on earth. Jewish followers of Jesus Christ, who was a Jew himself, saw him as the Messiah and considered him to be a spiritual saviour and the son of God. So Christianity and Judaism have the same roots. They both use the Old Testament of the Bible, which includes the 10 Commandments, as a source of inspiration and guidance.

Christianity believes in a single God, although "He" is represented in the trilogy of Father, Son and Holy Ghost. Christians also pray to numerous saints, foremost among them the Virgin Mary, using them as intermediaries and advocates in their access to God. Faithful Christians believe that salvation leading to eternal spiritual life in heaven is the reward given by God to those who have lived good lives, while unrepentant sinners are consigned to spend eternity in a state of perdition.

Islam is thought by its adherents to have been in existence since time immemorial. It has slowly been revealed to man by a succession of prophets including Abraham, Moses and Jesus, all of whom are revered by Muslims. Without doubt, the most important prophet of Islam is Mohammed, who lived from 570-632 AD.

Although Mohammed had always followed a spiritual lifestyle, it was when he was 40 years old that an angel spoke to him and gave him the word of Allah. The messages which he received from the angel on that and subsequent occasions were written down. These and other earlier writings form the Islamic holy book, the Qur'an. It is interesting that about one third of the Qur'an has writings which are also to be found in the Bible. Moreover, it is the same Archangel Gabriel who is accepted as God's messenger in Judaism, Christianity and Islam.

Muslims believe that there is only one God who is all knowing and all powerful. Those who truly believe and adhere to the requirements of Islam will, after death, live forever in happiness and comfort while those who do not believe will suffer eternally in hell.

Scholars frequently make reference to the Judaeo-Christian roots of teaching and culture or, more comprehensively, the Abrahamic religions which includes Islam. If, however, we are to look at the origins of Judaism, Christianity and Islam, we find that they are all claim the city of Jerusalem. Important sites for all three religions are, quite literally, architecturally and archaeologically, layered one on top of the other. A thousand years before the birth of Christ, the Temple of Jerusalem was built as the focal point of Judaism. For Christians, the same site is believed to be exact place on which the crucifixion took place. For Muslims, Jerusalem is considered to be their third most holy city because it is the site of the Al-Aqsa mosque.

Given the amount of religious intolerance in the world, what is truly striking is the similarity between all of the main religions, with the possible exception of Buddhism which does not have a god. Hinduism, Judaism, Christianity and Islam all believe in a single all powerful God. All of these religions as well as some branches of Buddhism believe in some form of life after death.

In the United States, a school class of eight year olds were asked to write a letter to God. One letter said, "Dear God, I am an American, what are you?" Even at that age there is a sense that God does or should conform to our identity. It is unthinkable that He could be different. That is why a middle-eastern Jewish Jesus Christ is so often portrayed in Europe as a blonde European. In whichever part of the world we are, we seem to be able to take quite literally the phrase that God created man in his own image. Therefore God looks like us, whatever we ourselves look like.

A common theme in most religions and throughout time has been a requirement to suffer mentally and physically in order to expiate our sins and receive divine acceptance. Christianity, like many religions, has tended to look at the beliefs and practices of other faiths with a dismissive abhorrence. Yet to followers of some Eastern religions, the Catholic concept of original sin seems incredibly bizarre and contrived. As the Reverend Peter Owen

Jones said, "*Why does finding God have to be all about suffering? Why can't it be about enjoying a lovely day?*" By extension, one might ask why is God so obscure? Why can't he be visible and accessible to all, thus avoiding the confusion?

All religions advocate tolerance and understanding, yet all religions – with the possible exception of Buddhism – have displayed the complete opposite and practised incarceration, terrible torture and the fighting of wars, all in the name of defending and promoting their own faith. How can Christians who follow a Jewish Jesus be anti-Semitic? How can Muslims whose faith is built on the love of tolerance and beauty reject out of hand the faith held by anyone who is not Islamic? Is religious tolerance an oxymoron? It would appear that the more fervently religious an individual or society is, the less tolerant they are. Instead, the major religions, and certainly different denominations within each religion, should concentrate on what unites them, remembering the universal injunction to love thy neighbour.

Whatever faith we choose, it should most certainly incorporate acceptance of our fellow man and a genuine attempt to understand and tolerate those whose beliefs and practices differ from our own.

It was a wise man and true believer in God, the Muslim leader Akbar the Great who said, "*God does not mind the name by which we call Him.*"

SPIRITUALITY

In Western society, many people say that they are not religious but that they are spiritual. I remember telling a friend that I did not understand what people meant by spirituality. He looked at me in astonishment and said that he thought that I was one of the most spiritual people he knew. That gave me a nice warm feeling, a sense that I was not missing out on this highly prized gift which people refer to as spirituality. It did not, however, answer my question as to what spirituality actually is.

Is the concept of spirituality outside a religious context suspect or desirable? Is it a "pick and mix" version of beliefs which allows us to take those we that we like, while at the same time ignoring the responsibilities associated with orthodox religion? Having our own private concept of forces for both good and evil allows us to choose what is acceptable and desirable for us. We can even decide for ourselves whether or not there is any post-mortal reckoning, which will yield punishment or reward. It allows us to have it both ways, rather like the prayer St. Augustine purportedly offered up following his conversion to Christianity, which said, "*Lord please grant me a life of abstinence and celibacy – but not yet.*"

So let me ask you the question: *What does spirituality mean to you?* Before you continue to read, write down your answer.

I deliberately set out to ask many people what spirituality meant to them. The majority of people replied in one of two ways. The first was to give, what for me, was an in-concise, obscure and unintelligible answer. Others talked about experiences which to them were spiritual. Experiences which were preternatural and emotionally enriching in an inexplicable way.

Neale Donald Walsh wrote in his bestseller, "Conversations with God – Book Two", "*Religion encourages you to explore the thoughts of others and accept them as your own. Spirituality invites you to toss away the thoughts of others and come up with your own.*"

Echoing this sentiment, an Anglican priest told me that he was pleased to be retired. Now, he said, he could express his own beliefs rather than merely regurgitate church doctrine.

David N. Elkins at Pepperdine University developed a definition of spirituality that focuses on the human experience of spirituality that says, "*Spirituality, which comes from the Latin spiritus, "meaning breath of life," is a way of being and experiencing that which comes from awareness of a transcendental dimension and that is characterized by certain identifiable values in regard to self, others, nature, life and whatever one considers to be the Ultimate.*"

Another definition from Simon King-Spooner states, "*By spirituality, I mean something like this: an encompassing 'significance' or 'meaning' within which our lives are lived, wittingly or unwittingly; which surrounds us at every hand if only we let ourselves be open to it; with which, anyway, our day-to-day experience is far more saturated than we realize; and against which all other significances and meanings are of a lower order, except insofar as they reach towards the greater significance that contains them.*"

A friend wrote, "*I think that it is difficult to use language to define spirituality, as the essence of spirituality cannot be pinned down in language, it can only be hinted at, or alluded to. Language depends on our own conceptual systems. Perhaps it is better to describe our own main spiritual experiences in the hope that it will strike a harmonious chord with the listener. For example, some moments in love-making could be described as spiritual.*"

So too could be the wonderful experiences we occasionally encounter in nature and mysteriously find epiphanic. Incredibly beautiful sunsets, the star-studded sky only seen in isolated locations or the wonder of a harvest moon.

Perhaps, like so many things in life, we over-complicate our understanding of the universal feeling which we call spirituality. It is transcendental and simply refers to a thinking process beyond the empirical and material; a case of heart rather than mind. In spirituality, we bypass logic and react with pure emotion. We are refreshed, inspired and enthralled by emotions which move us in an unexpected way and can at times cause us to react with unbridled and inexplicable joy.

Humour makes us laugh because it catches us by surprise. It juxtaposes our expectations with something entirely different. Could it be that spirituality works in the same way? We move beyond the mundane and ordinary into the realm of awe and wonder. We take comfort from the beauty of the natural world sensing that nature is sublime, and that we are both integral to it and in complete harmony with it.

PRAYER AND MEDITATION

In theistic religions, prayer is used to honour, thank and worship God as well as to communicate with "Him." To be open to hearing the word of God and to speak to "Him" directly. The belief that God knows us completely and intimately is comforting. Who among us would not want an intimate connection with someone, or something omnipotent who knows, loves and cares for us?

Yet if Buddhists do not believe in God, then to whom do they pray and for what purpose? Moreover, if Buddhists pray and gain benefit from doing so, then so also can anyone, including agnostics and atheists.

The answer is that Buddhists believe in an abstract principle of goodness. They believe that people form their own idea of God in a less formalised way than in a religion such as Christianity. Herein lies the problem for anyone brought up in or trained from childhood in a theistic religion.

Buddhist prayer does not petition a superior power in the hope or anticipation of changing circumstances. It is somewhat circular in that the listener or recipient is the same person who is praying. It is a form of meditation. It is a cleansing of the mind which removes negativity and replaces it with positive thinking.

Buddhists believe that it is our own thought processes which create the world in which we live. Given that our lives are governed by our perceptions, there is a great deal to commend this thinking. If Buddhists constantly think about spreading peace and goodness in the world, it is far more likely to occur. Sadly, the opposite is also true. In societies and religions, both Western and

Eastern, which seek control over others, especially if they use force and coercion to achieve this control, they will perpetuate the cycle of violence.

We all have a choice of whether or not to set aside time in order to pray and meditate. We all have the opportunity to cleanse our thoughts and to spend time thinking about the goodness and beauty which we can find in the people around us and in nature itself. It forms a wonderful counterbalance to the rush and stresses we impose on ourselves in daily life.

Prayer in a theistic religion is well understood and frequently proscribed. In Buddhism, there is a blending of prayer and meditation. So what is meditation when it is practised alone? To start with, let's clarify a couple of things. Meditation is not the sole preserve of Indian holy men or "new age" commune dwellers. Meditation is also practised by a whole range of people in the West, from Wall Street traders to British homemakers. In fact, the latter group sometimes practice meditation without putting that name to it. Anyone who participates in a yoga classes will know that these include a "quiet time," which is a form of meditation.

Within walking distance of my home there is the parkland surrounding an old mansion. In the UK, affluent families have always built wonderful houses in the most beautiful places. Successive generations have often changed both the house and even the landscaping, but the reason why that location was originally chosen always remains – there is natural beauty there. In "my" parkland there are public pathways running across the pasture fields, so it is legally open to anyone. What surprises me is how few people I ever see on my frequent walks. Roads are crowded and supermarkets are packed, but this place of complete tranquillity is almost unused.

I know that when I walk in this area I will feel uplifted. Despite having been there hundreds of times, it seems to me that the weather and the lighting are never quite the same. Every tree in the rolling landscape is very familiar to me but I always see the park in a fresh way and it never ceases to give me pleasure. When I am alone, I walk quite quickly up the first hill. I am thankful that my body is fit and truly rejoice in my ability, both physically and mentally, to see this beauty. This for me is a form of renewal. This for me is a form of meditation.

Other people have said that pottering in their garden, which involves planting things, nurturing them and watching them grow is their ultimate form of contemplation and relaxation. Anyone lucky enough to have been snorkelling over coral reefs will know how absolutely mesmerising this can be. Coral grows in such a variety of shapes and colours, ranging from the subtle to the psychedelic. If you then add to this a profusion of tropical fish, the mind is so captivated that it cannot drift to more mundane things. Finally, the sound of breathing through a snorkel is magnified when the head is underwater. So the slow, rhythmic sound of our own breath adds to the hypnotic and meditative sensation.

Definitions for meditation vary but there is one common objective. That is the body should be without tension, which in turn allows the mind to engage deliberately in contemplation. Buddhists talk about taming the "monkey mind" which jumps and swings from one thing to another in a state of over-activity. Teachers of meditation have the same goal but take a slightly different approach. They hope to achieve renewed energy by allowing the mind to relax completely.

To avoid unwanted thoughts by allowing them to come and go. They are just thoughts which are allowed to pass un-judged. If we allow our eyes to go into soft focus, we relax. The opposite is the concentrated gaze we have when we are tense. The meditator may deliberately dwell on something which is happening right now. They may focus all their attention on a candle flame, noting its colour, how it flickers and changes. Or they may focus on their own breath, studying every detail about it, as they draw in and exhale.

In its simplest terms, meditation allows us to take a break

from the endless range of issues which occupy our thoughts, and in so doing tire and exhaust us. It allows us to deliberately think about beautiful and loving things, to be renewed and regenerated through mental rest from our generally debilitating thoughts. Meditation gives us the chance to focus on the state we wish to be in, rather than merely eliminating that which we do not want.

Formal meditation, as opposed to "walking in the park meditation," concentrates on the present. Any thoughts of the past or future are gently ignored. As with any unwanted thoughts that enter the mind of the meditator, their presence is acknowledged before they are gently set aside.

Joyce Grenfell had a lovely line about living in the present. She said, *"There is only this minute – and I'm in it!"*

When we are tired, either emotionally or physically, most of us think about trying to sleep. Even Shakespeare thought sleep was the answer when, in Macbeth, he wrote, *"Sleep which knits up the ravelled sleeve of care."* People who are used to meditating take quite a different view. They find much greater restoration and renewed energy through the process of meditation. This is easy to explain when we remember the fact that even during sleep our minds continue to be very active. We continue subconsciously to think about our problems and launch off into the realm of dreams, some of which can be emotionally taut and disturbing.

Many years ago I used to travel to the Far East with groups of businessmen on extended trips which could last for up to three weeks. The work and travel were exhausting for most of us but one man seemed not to get tired. He was an ethnic Indian who, despite living in Europe, continued his practice of meditation. Although he was in his 70s and a good deal older than the rest of us, he exuded good health and energy.

When I asked him about this, he attributed all of his physical and mental well-being to his meditation. He told me that wherever he was in the world or whatever he had been doing, he would always get out of bed at 5 a.m. He would then meditate for two hours. The amount of sleep he had had prior to 5 a.m. seemed almost irrelevant. His energy and vitality came from his meditation.

Anyone who is interested in learning to meditate can do so. There are many books devoted to meditation and there are numerous courses which are accessible to most people.

There is much in common between prayer, meditation and self-hypnosis. Whatever form this wonderful process takes, and however it is achieved, it offers everyone renewal and the ultimate sanctuary.

ATHEISM

"Today there is a contentment in people's lives. They don't see the need for another dimension" – Kevin Mullen, a Catholic Priest.

Atheists, like everyone else, will have been exposed to all of the world's great religions and quite possibly will have received some instruction in one of them, probably in their childhood. They too will have asked the question, is there a God? They too will have asked the question, is there eternal life involving a heaven or a hell?

Atheists are not usually iconoclasts, nor have they merely fallen into spiritual lassitude. They have simply reached the conclusion that there is no God, and that when we die it is quite literally the end for us. The philosopher A. C. Grayling describes death as being the same as before we were born. That is, we did not exist before we were born and we will not exist after the death.

Atheists genuinely feel that religious belief is a simplistic way of denying our own mortality, a desperate search for certainty in an uncertain world. That believing in both God and an afterlife, which includes a heavenly state, is wishful thinking. Atheists believe that for most people Darwin's theory of evolution has satisfactorily explained the creation of man, without the involvement of a deity.

Perhaps in response to the concept of atheism, Canon John Oates said, *"Those of us who are logical and rational do not believe in angels. The problem with this is that we are, therefore, unable to hear what they have to say to us."*

Any person who believes in God has the capacity also to

believe in the Devil and indeed a host of other supernatural powers. G K Chesterton wrote, "*When people start believing in God they do not believe in one thing, they believe in anything.*"

There is no doubt that many people, especially those who are poor and without influence, find comfort and solace in religious belief. Karl Marx described religion as "*the opiate of the masses.*" For some people, God and religion give a ready-made purpose in life. Without this, it is necessary to find our own purpose for existing. Some people find security through their connection with other people, others find security in money and some people find security in religion. One staunch Catholic was said by someone who knew her well to be so self-absorbed with preparing for the next life that she was barely participating in this one.

The word "religion" comes from the stem "religere" which means to gather up into a group. So religion is belonging to a group or community. Atheists can also enjoy participation in groups and community. They simply reject that the notion that there is a divine, controlling force. Paradoxically, people may be drawn to religion in order to offset psychological imbalances created in their youth by religion. For example, anyone who feels overwhelming or inappropriate guilt, especially relating to sex, may turn to religion in order to assuage this guilt and find absolution. Woody Allen said in one of his movies, "*Everyone knows the same truth, the only difference is how we choose to distort it.*"

An example of religious distortion and pragmatism was exhibited by missionaries in the Canadian far north. They found that threatening sinners with a burning hell did not deter their congregation. On the contrary, as they found this idea of perpetual warmth quite appealing, missionaries changed their picture of hell for the Inuit peoples to a state of permanent and intense cold.

The majority of holy texts and religious preaching start with the assumption that those reading or listening already believe in the existence of God. They have since childhood just accepted the existence of God as a fact, or chosen to make that "giant leap of faith." This in turn leads to religious argument which is often far too convoluted and abstract. Yet the big questions for which human beings seek answers are quite simple.

How did the universe start? What existed before the universe? We find it impossible to understand the concept of complete nothingness – that is, not even empty space existing. Given that mankind does exist, what if any purpose is there for our existence?

The post-Darwinian theory is that life started accidentally in a complicated chemical mixture colloquially described as the "primordial soup." Cambridge science professor and practising Christian, Colin Humphries is comfortable with this theory saying that, "*If life emerged from a primeval soup, then God was the master chef.*"

Whether we as human beings like it or not, we are genetically very closely related to pigs. Moreover, we have more than a mere resemblance to apes. We are apes and share 98.5% of our DNA with chimpanzees. Atheists certainly do not believe that animals, which include human beings, have souls or exist in any way following their death other than by the influence that they generated during their lifetime.

Intelligence involves the capacity for "self-awareness." Man is not alone among the animal kingdom for having self-awareness. Dolphins have a high level of self-awareness and are able to recognize themselves in a mirror. To a lesser extent many other animals including cats and dogs have some self-awareness. It is human self-awareness, enhanced by the development of language and imagination, which has led all mankind since the first bipedal hominids to develop the concept of God. Atheists say that God did not create man. Man created God. And it is man that has put words into the mouth of God.

PREPARING FOR DEATH

For the majority of people, their greatest fear is death. In reality, it is a fear of what lies beyond death. It is a fear either of the unknown or, worse still, of some anticipated form of purgatory. Regardless of our beliefs, it is certainly the ultimate change.

If we are lucky, we will go through old age before we die. Or perhaps what I should really say is that, if we are lucky, we will go through a worthwhile old age – that is, we will remain active both physically and mentally. We will be able to enjoy and value this stage of our lives. It may be the first time in our life when we are actually the person we always wanted to be. The actor Ian Richardson clearly felt this in his late 60s. When writing about his youth, he described it *"as a time full of unfulfilled ambitions and undefined aspirations."*

What we do not want in old age is to deteriorate in mind and body to the point where our own dementia frightens us, and our lives are a meaningless burden to others. Another old actor said, *"life is a pretty good play but with a poorly written third act."*

There is much we can do to improve the third act. For a start, we can forget about retirement. That does not mean we should continue working at the same occupation that we have been in all our lives. On the contrary, this is an opportunity to explore a whole range of fresh new options. To do all of the things that we wanted to do but were not free to pursue. To travel, to be creative, to socialise more (not less) and to experiment with a range of new interests. Human biology is such that the more interested and involved we are in life, the healthier we remain. The more pleasure we experience in life, the stronger our immune system becomes.

The veteran war correspondent and broadcaster, Sir Charles Wheeler, spent his 68th birthday being bombarded by mortar fire in the ruins of a burned-out hotel in Kuwait during the 1991 Gulf war. His comment was, *"I can't believe how lucky I am to be here. Something awful might have happened to me – like retirement."*

Probably the most painful emotional experience, and greatest sadness, that any of us will suffer, will result from the death of someone we love. The irrevocability of this loss can seem unbearable. Yet we fully understand that all human beings die. We know that all the people we love are going to die, and we also know that we ourselves will die.

When we delight at the birth of baby, we do so in the knowledge that life is transitory. We know that there will come a time when this life will also end. Unless a child is sick, however, we do not think about their death. In part, this may be because, in all likelihood, we will predecease them and therefore not witness their death. They will carry the baton of life into an unknown future of which we will not be a part. We enjoy watching them grow through the various stages of childhood and anticipate all of the good things in life we hope they will encounter. We rightly focus on life and all of the positive things which drive us forward and give us pleasure. The problem is that we spend so much time working on the basis that everyone's life is ongoing that we do not prepare ourself and others for the inevitability of death.

The preparation we can sensibly undertake involves our relationship with those people who are most likely to die, the elderly and the infirm.

Similarly, we can prepare for our own death.

Logically, most people do not do this until they perceive themselves to be getting old and therefore getting closer to death. While life today is less uncertain than at any time in the past, death does still come quickly or unexpectedly to some people, and that could include us. Our preparation for death should primarily be concerned about the emotional aspects of loss, but at the same time there are practicalities involving the changes which are the inevitable consequence of death.

Setting aside for a moment the emotional aspects, we should ask ourselves what the practical implications would be in the event of our death or disability. How would our family cope financially? Do we have a sufficient amount of life and disability insurance? Have we granted someone Enduring Power of Attorney? Have we got a Will which reflects our wishes and current circumstances? Without a legally acceptable Will, and especially in cases of "common law" and same sex relationships, it is possible that assets may not be passed on in the way that we would anticipate, or want.

If we were to die suddenly, do those people who would be responsible for our funeral know what our wishes are? Have we ever discussed these, or better still, written them down? Would our next of kin easily know where to find all the information they would require, ranging from our bank and other financial details to house deeds and car ownership documents? Although the time of death is one of emotional turmoil, the practicalities of life, such as paying bills, go on. There will, in fact, be increased expenses arising from the funeral itself. All this at a time when bank accounts may be frozen pending probate.

Are there any letters or documents which we would like people to find quickly? Are there any documents which we would not want anyone to see and that we would be better off disposing of now? Are there any loose ends in our life?

I know one man who had a life-long, loving relationship, outside his marriage. He left a letter with his solicitor addressed to this woman, which was to be mailed after his death.

Prior to his death from cancer in 1996, the journalist Martyn Harris brought his own life into focus when he wrote, "*The gossamer stuff of ambition, money and possessions fade away in times of crisis. The real structure of life is then seen to be wife, children, family and friends.*"

The death of other people raises many questions, doubts and concerns as well as reminding us of our own pending mortality. For the religious, there is the questioning of faith. "How could God allow this to happen?" For some of us, there is a sense that the pain is so great that we feel our own life has effectively come to an end. The widower who felt so deeply when he changed the message on his answering machine from, "we are sorry that we are not able to take your call at this time," to "I am sorry that I am unable to take your call at this time." He said that it felt like the ultimate dismissal of his wife. Sometimes we want to hold on to the grief. To allow it to pass is like a betrayal of the bond we had.

When someone close to us dies, we lose at least one of our roles in life. The role of a son or daughter, the role of brother, sister, friend or, perhaps worst of all, that of a parent. Losing a spouse or partner means we have to reinvent ourselves. We are no longer half of a couple. We are again single. A role for which we may no longer be prepared. As if the emotional burden of grief was not great enough, this in turn has the potential to lead to further problems. At a time when our emotional defences are at their lowest, we may also suffer from the related effects of physical illness, ranging from a weakened immune system to psychosomatic ailments.

Each of us individually has to find our way through the process of mourning in a way that is meaningful to us. There is no single formula which works for everyone but this is certainly a time when the support of friends and community can help considerably. This is also a time to avoid the seductively easy options of drinking too much, sleeping too much and withdrawing from real people into the apparently comforting glow of the television.

There have been occasions when someone I did not know particularly well has died. On these occasions, it is very easy to ignore the situation and say that it does not really affect us. It does, however, affect those close to the person who died. It is important that they should hear from us, that they should receive even the most modest support and comfort which comes from our acknowledgement of their loss and sadness.

We usually assume that there is only sadness related to death. Sometimes there is also relief. A sense of relief that the person who has died is no longer suffering. A sense of relief for us that our worrying about the person we loved is now over. The first time I understood this was at the reception following the funeral of a friend whom I remembered as being highly intelligent, witty, urbane and charming. In their tastefully decorated, art-filled Edinburgh flat, I was amazed when his widow calmly told me that she was pleased that her husband was now dead. Remembering that I had not seen my friend for a couple of years, I quickly had to put this remark into the context of the terrible decline he had suffered as a result of Alzheimer's disease.

We can be in a close relationship with someone and yet be indifferent to their death. In Ibsen's play, "A Dolls House," an impoverished widow says of her negligent husband, *"He left me nothing, not even a sense of loss."*

We can love someone and also be angry that they died. Like the woman who was widowed at fifty by a husband who was a life-long smoker and died of lung cancer. We can be angry that a lack of suitable preparation before someone's death has left us in difficult circumstances. Sometimes a spouse's premature death leaves the remaining partner feeling that they are too young to give up on life but too old start again. A child may well feel anger towards a parent they loved dearly if that parent died under accidental or health-related circumstances, which could have been avoided.

Unless we commit suicide, we do not have any control over the final timing and circumstances of our death. One man used to joke that he wanted to be shot dead by a jealous husband when he was 96. If I could choose the perfect death for myself it would be something like this. After a long, healthy, active and happy life, I would attend some large family gathering at which I would see all of those people who are most dear to me. Then during the night I would silently pass away. No long debilitating illness, no substantial loss of my senses or faculties, and certainly no pain.

The renowned photographer Richard Avedon achieved a more or less perfect end to his life. He continued to do what he enjoyed most until the day he died. He was still working on assignments until the age of 81. A chance comment by a work colleague led him to remark, "If something happens to me, I'm ready to go." Shortly afterwards, he died quickly from an aneurysm in the brain. To have lived a fulfilling life, be "ready to go" and then die quickly is a wonderful formula.

For the majority of people, old age and death is not like this. The senses do weaken for a variety of reasons. Our strength and mobility do diminish. Worst of all is that many of us will suffer from disease which will cause a slow and painful degeneration towards an uncomfortable death. The book "Tuesdays with Morrie" written by Mitch Albom is the true account of an old man's stoical but sad decline. What he fears most is the impending indignity. He dreads the day when "I can no longer wipe my own arse."

In extreme cases, there are people who suffer for years from the most agonising conditions. Many of these people simply become tired of the physical and mental burden caused by their illness. For them, there is no enjoyment in life, only pain, and they no longer wish to defer death.

In the United States, the late Admiral Chester Nimitz Jr and his wife had for many years rationally discussed what they would do if they reached this stage of life. The outcome was that in 2002, when they were both elderly, 86 and 89 respectively, and incurably ill (Chester had congestive heart failure and his wife had bone-snapping advanced osteoporosis), they decided to end their lives together. The devoted couple had prepared the method of their death, sleeping pills, well in advance and died entirely in a manner and at the timing of their choice. They themselves exited this world as they wished to. They withdrew from life before their dignity faltered and before they lost the physical and mental ability to control their remaining time. Because they had openly discussed this for a long time with their children, as well as their doctor and lawyer, there was no criticism of their family and no question of any legal action being taken. More importantly, there was no reason for anyone to feel guilt in this matter.

The letter left by Chester Nimitz on the day of their death reads as follows, "*Our decision was made over a considerable period of time and was not carried out in acute desperation. Nor is it the expression of a mental illness. We have consciously, rationally, deliberately and of our own free will taken measures to end our lives today because of the physical limitations on our quality of life placed upon us by age, failing vision, osteoporosis, back and painful orthopaedic problems.*"

This is in no way encouraging or condoning a casual approach to depression-induced suicide or unregulated euthanasia. But for some people, including those with the courage and foresight of Admiral and Mrs. Nimitz, the circumstances of their death can also be a matter of choice.

Former British politician, Michael Portillo, undertook exhaustive research on the most humane way to carry out the death penalty, in jurisdictions where this is still carried out. His aim was not to support the principle of the death penalty but to promote the idea that if societies are to kill human beings, they should do so in the most acceptable way.

What he found was that the vast majority of ways in which people are killed are painful and distressing, both to the victim and to the witnesses. A conclusion of his research found that a humane way of animal slaughter was the administering of nitrogen gas. This caused hypoxia, the elimination of oxygen in the blood stream, which in turn led to a brief state of euphoria followed within fifteen seconds by unconsciousness. Death then occurs within a minute. As a method of suicide or assisted suicide, this seems more reliable and preferable to almost any other.

Of the many mistakes that I have made in my life so far, the one that I regret most is my ignorance and lack of understanding prior to and during the illness which led to my wife's death. I can still vividly remember my own shock when the doctor told me that my wife's abdominal pain was the result of a pancreatic tumour. It felt as if the blood quite literally drained out of me. I was suddenly pale and felt very cold and shaky, despite the warmth in the over-heated hospital.

The specialist advised me not to tell my wife what he had found while she was coming out of the anaesthetic. Rather, he would tell her the following day. Perhaps this is when the whole process of deception began. It was certainly right to be optimistic and to look for the best outcome. But this turned into a two-year process of apparent denial or deception by me, and by my wife herself, aided and abetted by a factory medical system.

The surgeon who was to undertake the removal of the tumour was professional and kindly. He did warn me that "the plumbing in this part of the body" was quite complicated and that there was a 5% chance that she would not make it through the operation. So within 10 days our lives had changed from dull routine into the fear of cancer and even a 5% chance of immediate death.

My wife did survive the operation. Within hours of her regaining consciousness in the intensive care unit, I remember the enormous happiness I felt. My wife was so buoyant and elated. She was joking with the staff and insisting that the doctor in charge should release her to go home. It was as if the very essence of my wife's strong personality, happiness and optimism was bursting out. She was powerfully alive at this time and I was probably happier then than at any other time in my life. She was euphoric and so was I. My euphoria came from the fact that I not only had my wife back but even had an intensified version of her. Her euphoria must have been a celebration that she was alive, but was also fuelled by the cocktail of anaesthetic barbiturates still washing through her system.

What followed was a roller coaster of highs and lows. We were told that the operation was completely successful but there

215

was a "chance" that some cancer cells had got into the lymph system. For this reason, it would be necessary to start a program of chemotherapy. Despite having private medical coverage, the consultant oncologist to whom we were assigned was arrogant and rude. Consultations with him were never private, there were always several other people in the room, none of whom were introduced and whose role was never explained. The consultant's performance appeared to be far more concerned with impressing these acolytes with his genius, omnipotence and invulnerability than with the sensitive care of his patient.

There was an ongoing cycle of hospital visits, blood tests and the prescribing of a variety of drugs to combat the variety of symptoms. The hardest symptom to deal with was the pain. Towards the end of her illness, I was administering diamorphine to my wife. It was up to me to control her pain, yet at the same time not give her so much that she ceased to participate in life. For someone with no medical training and no experience in these matters, it was a major challenge.

Lack of experience is the real core off this issue. My wife was a person of great courage. That is not the same as being fearless. She, like all of us, felt fear but her courage and determination meant that she would not yield to fear. She was absolutely determined to win her battle with cancer and to survive into normal old age. For this reason, she pressed on with orthodox cancer treatment and at the same time studied complementary procedures.

I remember the day when, in the Royal Marsden Hospital, London's leading cancer hospital, she was told that the cancer had moved to her liver and that there was nothing more they could do for her. Her first reaction was to ask if she could she get a liver transplant. When this was denied, she started to see a Harley Street doctor who practised alternative medicine. This involved an extremely strict diet which caused her to lose weight, and in my opinion, may in fact have shortened her lifespan.

Throughout this time, she never even mentioned the prospect

of death. I was complicit in this denial, even after I was sure that her illness was terminal. I wanted her to live with hope. Moreover, knowing how much longer someone will live, or to be more direct, when they will die, is always imprecise. Having said that, I do believe that I could have been given a more medically calculated and realistic appraisal.

So what was the point of these lies and self-deception? I thought that my wife wanted and needed to believe that she would overcome her illness. Close friends have said that she was trying to protect me, that she was trying to keep my spirits high. Our family doctor told me later that he thought it was Sue's way of dealing with the whole situation. I can understand why he would think this, but knowing my wife's incredible bravery, I do not think that was the situation. The net result was that two strong people, whose relationship together had been absolutely the most important and valuable part of each of their lives, were playing games and deceiving each other.

If I could turn the clock back, what would I have done differently? I think the answer would have been to honestly face reality right from the beginning – to accept that my wife had a serious illness. While being as optimistic as possible, still addressing the reality that this could result in her premature death. Simply having opened that line of conversation and communication would have eliminated the collaborative lies and changed everything. It would have kept intact the direct and loving honesty we had always shared.

When several parts of her liver were affected by the cancer, an honest approach by both of us would have allowed us to settle into a calmer level of acceptance. This in turn would have allowed us to rejoice in the wonderful things we had done together. To look through the photo albums, remembering struggles we faced together as well as all those happy times we shared. To laugh together celebrating the 30 years of love, friendship and companionship we had given each other. I wish that I had given her far more touch. Loving touch to her face and hands. Touch that would have said so much more than words. Touch that would have comforted so much more words.

I would like to have apologised to her for the times when I behaved badly. I would like to have apologised for the mistakes I made. For both our sakes, I would like to have given her the chance to forgive me. I would like her to have said to me whatever she may have wanted to say. She no doubt thought that we knew each other so well, that her feelings, wants and desires did not need to be expressed. This was true, but still I would like to have heard them said rather than merely being assumed and implied. Most of all, I would like to have told her many more times how very much I loved her.

A couple of years after Sue's death, one of our sons said that he would give anything to have a good long chat with his mother. I too feel the same way. There would be so much to talk about now; so much catching up to do. After a person's death, we love them in a different way. Thomas Hardy's first wife Emma had been the passion of his youth, but it was only after her death that he rediscovered the strength of his love for her.

The outside world saw my wife as strong and outspoken. What perhaps only I and our sons saw was her vulnerability and her gentleness. I often thought of her as being like a female eider duck which would pluck down from her own breast, in order to line the nest and in so doing would selflessly provide warmth and comfort for her family.

If, miraculously, my wife returned now she would get a much better man in me than she left behind. A man who now appreciates how much physical work she did, what a great burden she always carried. A man more willing and able to share her load. A man more capable of giving her greater love and appreciation. A man who has leaned the basics of cooking and now knows how to operate the washing machine. A man who has acquainted himself with the dubious pleasures of housework after learning that the lavatory is not self-cleaning.

What have I really learnt from this experience that I can use in the rest of my life or that could be of value to anyone else? It is that hiding from the reality of death does not achieve anything. We all try to be successful in the way we lead our life. We can also try to be successful in the way that we cope with impending death. Long before we, or the people we love, are close to death, we should be making preparations for the time when we are separated. Not in a morbid debilitating way but in a positive, joyous and celebratory way. In a way that prevents future regrets and remorse.

I wish that my wife had left me a letter, preferably hand written, saying all the things that she knew I would like to have heard her say. References to the things that we both loved, such as our sons, and to the things that made us laugh together, like our much loved and characterful old cat. Even now, it is comforting when I see her handwriting in the inscription in a book. How much better if she had left me a loving farewell note. This is something we can all do. We can take the time to write letters to those people who will still have a need or desire for some type of connection with us after we are gone. A tangible reminder of a loving bond; an acknowledgement that death can never take away the love.

Actually, love is what it is all about. There is a remarkable 600 year old tomb in Chichester Cathedral. On top of this "table tomb" are the stone carved effigies of the Earl and Countess of Arundel, he wearing full armour and she elegantly dressed. What is remarkable about these effigies is that the Earl is shown as having removed the gauntlet from his right hand. His wife Eleanor is depicted as leaning slightly on her left side extending her right hand into his. In an age when men like this did not show any emotion, holding her hand for eternity was a truly significant sign of affection.

It was this tomb which inspired Philip Larkin to write a well-known poem about death. The line which is most often quoted is the last one which says, *"What will survive of us is love."*

In our own time, we have seen the horror of the terrorist

attacks which took place in America on "Nine-Eleven." When people knew that they were about to die they used mobile phones or any means possible to do what was most important to them – to tell the people closest to them how much they loved them.

I believe very much in the value and ritual of the funeral. It can, of course be argued that the person who has died has no awareness of this event. When Marilyn Monroe died, her former husband, the playwright Arthur Miller, was asked why he would not attend the funeral. He simply said, "Because Marilyn won't be there."

It is quite a good exercise for any of us to think about what would happen if we died suddenly. Who would arrange our funeral? Would they do it in a way that we would like? Who would actually make the effort to attend our funeral? Who would miss us and really care that we had died? It is because we can answer many of these questions that we can retain some peace and dignity as we approach death. If everyone merely opted for the Arthur Miller philosophy, no one would attend funerals, no one would remember us with kind words and our bodies might as well be conveyed to the dump on the back of a truck.

Funerals are for the benefit of the deceased and the living. They benefit the deceased in that we can all live with the knowledge that our bodies will be dealt with in a dignified, respectful and appropriate way. In the hauntingly beautiful Purcell opera "Dido and Aneas," Queen Dido, who is about to kill herself, sings the heart-rending lament "Remember Me." We all want those who love us and those whom we love to remember us. This is not arrogance and pride but it is a form of validation for our lives. It gives us the sense that our lives were significant to, and valued by, others. This too says, "Death where is thy sting?" and "Grave where is thy victory?"

More importantly, the ritual of the funeral allows those who are grieving to take the first transitional step towards accepting the loss of the relationship with the person who has died. The greater the love we felt, or the closer the relationship has been with the person who died, the more necessary it is to acknowledge the enormity of our loss.

When someone has been a major influence in our life, we cannot and do not wish to simply accept or dismiss the change of circumstance. As mourners, we need to acknowledge the importance of that person to our own lives. With a close family member whom we loved dearly, we need to be able to show and express our love. Our tears and heartache are a combination of sadness on behalf of the person who died, because their life is now over, and our own agonising sense of loss. We need the cathartic release that only the tears of mourning can give us.

Funeral services rightly give comfort to those in sorrow. Immediately after someone dies, we continue to feel their presence, perhaps with even greater intensity. We think about what they would be doing, saying or thinking in these circumstances. If we have been used to feeling someone's presence for many years, that feeling remains with us. In fact, because we are thinking about them so much at this time, we become even more aware of "feeling their presence." Is it this which gives rise to the optimistic hope or belief that some form of consciousness survives beyond physical death?

At my wife's funeral, I was of course sad and emotional. Outwardly, however, I was calm and controlled. It was up to me to ensure everything went smoothly and to give the large congregation the best address I could in order to honour my wife. About a month later, I attended the funeral of a business colleague who had died suddenly. His wife was calm and in control just as I had been. On the other hand, I, thinking about my wife and not being "on duty," could not stop myself from weeping. This funeral was the pin-prick which burst the massive emotional pressure which had built up inside me.

Poetry which we may have read before takes on a new poignancy and intensity when we hear those words read at a funeral. Sometimes these are the words we so desperately want to hear being said by the person who has died.

Canon Scott Henry Holland expressed this most beautifully when he wrote:

"Death is nothing at all.
I have only slipped away into the next room.
I am I, and you are you.
Whatever we were to each other, that we still are.
Call me by my old familiar name,
Speak to me in the easy way which you always used.
Put no difference in the tone,
Wear no forced air of solemnity of sorrow.
Laugh as we always laughed at the little jokes we enjoyed
together."

And Leo Marks wrote:

"The life that I have,
Is all that I have.
And the life that I have
Is yours.

"The love that I have,
Of the life that I have.
Is yours, and yours, and yours

"A sleep I shall have.
A rest I shall have.
Yet death will be but a pause.
For the peace of my years
In the long green grass
Will be yours, and yours, and yours."

Different religions have different beliefs, requirements and traditions concerning what happens to the body after death. Some Hindus require cremation and Muslims require burial. Christians traditionally used burial which was especially comforting in the past when people were less mobile. They usually lived close to the burial place of their parents and grandparents. Often they knew exactly where they themselves would be laid to rest.

Tombstone inscriptions are sometimes brief, merely giving factual information such as name, date of birth and the date of death. This shows us, even today, how short many lives were and still are. Epitaphs and more detailed inscriptions often give a vignette of the person who has died. The inscription is the opportunity to leave our final, not always loving thoughts, about that person literally carved in stone. Some tell a story, some are humorous and others are movingly sad.

"The children of Israel wanted bread
And the Lord sent them manna,
Old clerk Wallace wanted a wife,
And the devil sent him Anna."

John Dryden (1631-1700) wrote of his wife:

"Here lies my wife, here let her lie.
Now she's at rest, and so am I."

Humour both intentional and unintentional is sometimes found on headstones. The joke about the dentist filling his last cavity. Or the inscription which read, "Lord, she is thin." This was actually a spelling error by the stonemason who had meant to write, "Lord, she is Thine."

Or poignantly written on a young soldier's grave:

"Peacefully sleeping, free from pain
We would not wake you, to suffer again."

Perhaps saddest of all, on the eighteenth century grave of a young woman:

"Twenty years a maiden.
One year a wife,
One hour a mother,
Then I lost my life."

The final word of comfort, in which we must all believe, is that:

"Nothing dies that is remembered."

How we live our lives now will determine what inscription others will put over our grave.

As we progress in our understanding of life and move upwards on Maslow's pyramid, having built foundations and made choices, it is natural to want to express our feelings and reveal our appreciation of beauty.

LEVEL 6 – AESTHETIC NEEDS

Beauty, balance, form

CREATIVITY AND SELF-EXPRESSION

A key consideration is: What motivates us to be creative and yearn for self-expression? One element that gives us a sense of fulfilment is the degree to which we have been able to find self-expression.

This innate desire stems from the fact that we rightly believe that there is something unique and different about each of us. After all, no two people have had exactly the same experiences and therefore every person is genuinely unique. Self-expression is quite different to basic communication. When we communicate we are simply exchanging information. Self-expression goes far beyond mere communication, allowing us to explore our own circumstances and interpret our understanding and beliefs. Self-expression does not necessarily need an audience, whatever mode of self-expression we choose, whether singing in the bath or painting a landscape, it may well be for our own satisfaction alone.

Creativity and art, which are modes of self-expression, are interrelated but not the same thing. Whenever we bring components together and make something, we are quite literally being creative. If we assemble a garden shed, we are being creative. Producing art requires that we are creative, in the sense that there is an end product, but because art has no technological purpose it also implies that we have a higher purpose than pure functionality.

The key question is what motivates us to yearn for self-expression? It could be a simple matter of exploration, in which we are seeking our own individual answers. It could be a manifestation of one of the many facets of our ego which is looking for anything from danger, to exhibitionism, to pure pleasure. Or it could be that we feel we have some insight that we must share and impart. We all know the most obvious media for this expression which include music, architecture, writing, dance, theatre and painting. Perhaps Jean-Jacques Rousseau tried to answer this question when he said, "*The world of reality has its limits; the world of imagination is boundless.*"

There are things we will wish to express which are ineffable. The American artist Edward Hopper noted "*that if something can be said in words, why bother to paint it?*" Andy Wahol never explained his work, saying that it was futile to verbalise art. Daniel Barenboim said, "*Music is a wonderful escape but isn't just about sounds. If Beethoven's symphonies were only sounds, nobody would bother with them.*" A beautiful young cellist who had spent her entire life engrossed in music told me that she could not explain it. "*Music is a mystery,*" she said.

Even Paul Dirac, described at his funeral by Stephen Hawking as the greatest British theoretical physicist since Newton, never tried to explain his work to the uninitiated. Unlike Einstein, he never sought any form of public recognition. We either recognised and appreciated the purity of his equations or we did not.

Jeff Stewart, Head of New World Music, wrote that "*most people know instinctively that music has the power to soothe, relax, inspire and even heal. It calms us when we are stressed, can motivate us when we are dispirited and unlock our creative energies. Music makes us smile and makes us cry ... affects our bodies, minds and spirits ... it reaches deep into our very souls.*" As Alfred Lord Tennyson once observed, "*Music that gentler on the spirit lies, than tired eyelids upon tired eyes.*"

The biblical book of Exodus describes the ornate beauty of the Ark of the Covenant. Art in many forms is a gift to, and a recognition of, God. It has been said of the truly sublime music composed for the church by musicians such as Purcell, Brahms and Mozart that its beauty takes people into the presence of

God and allows them to see, feel and experience God's love. A cathedral chorister said that, *"Their singing was to the glory of God and to facilitate people in their worship."*

Self expression through creativity and artistic embellishment are to be found everywhere. The most practical shape for a dwelling is a simple box with a sloping roof which allows rain to run off it. But even the simple wooden peasants' homes in rural Russia are enriched with traditional fret work ornamentation. The roof of a medieval thatched cottage in England often had a pheasant or some other animal depicted in thatch, sitting on the roof as if it were real. Representing known forms of animals and people was probably the first type of self expression to be practised. Early man painted animals and hunting scenes on the walls of caves either to celebrate a successful hunt or in the hope that making such a depiction would encourage the spirits to ensure such an event would take place.

Art throughout the ages has been linked to the beliefs of the artist. Depicting various forms of fertility symbols and attempting to appease the powers of the universe have been a common theme in all forms of art. What is remarkable, given that the themes are so universal, is the endless variety of ways in which artists seek to find a fresh approach.

In the Western world, most of the great works of art created in the last millennium were inspired by religious belief. The passionate, emotive paintings of Giotto, Durer and Rembrandt. The great European cathedrals were born out of the idea, that man *"should build heaven on earth"* as suggested in the book of Revelation. These buildings, which are so impressive today, must have been totally awe inspiring when they were built with their wonderful stained-glass windows through which the congregation believed they could quite literally see the light of God.

Many people rightly believe that architecture is the only art form which is forced on all of us; we cannot help seeing the buildings around us. For this very reason, people throughout the ages have used architecture for self-aggrandisement and self-commemoration. The Roman Emperor Hadrian built numerous magnificent cities all of which cause us to remember him, and the grandeur of Versailles will forever be associated with Louis XIV.

Musical harmony, as well as the symmetry and balance of some architecture, like that of Andrea Palladio, confirm, enhance and reflect our innate desire for and belief in the principle of cosmic order.

Arguably the most beautiful building in the world, the Taj Mahal, once described by the poet Tagore as *"A tear drop on the cheek of time"* was built to honour and commemorate Shah Jahan's wife, Mumtaz. In more modest ways, we only have to look at the funerary architecture in cemeteries around the world to see that we do, quite literally, wish to have our names carved in stone.

Art is not always aesthetically beautiful. It can be an expression of that which fills us with horror such as Picasso's anti-war picture, Guernica. It is also frequently both historical and allegorical, as in the case of Goya's well-known painting entitled "The Third of May 1808," set following the Spanish uprising against Napoleon. In this horrific picture, we see terrible fear in the expression of a man as he faces a firing squad. What Goya is also saying to us is that we too are all looking down the gun barrel of time, towards our own certain death.

The art of a great writer is that it can carry us on a journey through the spectrum of human emotion. The miracle is that someone else's words can move us deeply and inspire us. Percy Shelley said, *"Poetry lifts the veil from the hidden beauty of the world, and makes familiar objects be as if they were not familiar."* Is there anyone who could remain unmoved by the power of William Blake's words:

Bring me my bow of burning gold!
Bring me my arrows of desire!
Bring me my spear! O clouds, unfold!
Bring me my chariot of fire!

All artists seek to express themselves in whatever medium works for them. The filmmaker Kevin Macdonald said that he found Nicolas Roeg, another filmmaker, to be *"Verbally inarticulate. Roeg's articulacy is purely visual. In his early films he developed an entire new (visual) language."*

The ballerina Uliana Lopatkina said that she *"Tries never to dance with just her body but with her soul and her heart."*

Claire Schrader, a drama therapist wrote, *"In Dionysian rites, participants reached an altered state known as ecstasis (from which the word ecstasy is derived) which enabled the release of powerful emotions through wild ecstatic expression."*

The desire for self expression is within us all. It is an exploration, and expression of ourselves, which is neither right nor wrong. An eight-year-old boy was asked why he liked singing. His reply was merely that he loses himself when he sings. A 15-year-old boy was asked why he liked drama. His reply was, "it allowed him to show feelings that he could not express at any other time or in any other way."

Our sense of self-fulfilment is dependent on our level of self-satisfaction relating to the achievements of our life. Self-expression can only be achieved when we have given sufficient thought to the world in general and to our own lives, to know what it is that we wish to express.

As we progress through life, we have the possibility to become the person we intrinsically are, giving full reign to our true identity. This, in turn, leads us to what Maslow calls self-actualisation.

LEVEL 7 – MOVING TOWARDS AND ACHIEVING SELF-ACTUALISATION

The Person We Are is the Person We Choose to Become

SOME FOREIGN WORDS TO THINK ABOUT

Getting the S&M balance right? When you hear someone say S and M, what do you immediately think of? Most people will think of sadomasochism. S&M reminds me of two completely different words. Two words which are not English, but the concepts of which are understood by us all. They are schadenfreude and mudita.

Although schadenfreude is a German word, it has counterparts in many other languages, but strangely not in English. We experience the emotion of schadenfreude when we take pleasure in someone else's misfortune. For example, if two men are playing golf together and one hits his ball into the rough, the second man, whatever he actually says, may be secretly pleased because he now has an advantage in the game.

Aggressive young business people clawing their way up the corporate ladder would no doubt be pleased when one of their rivals makes a mistake which puts them out of contention for promotion. To take an even stronger example, we understand when a country is at war that it is pleased by the death of thousands of the enemy.

Schadenfreude is generally considered to be passive. Something unfortunate occurs to someone else and we find pleasure in that misfortune. But wanting and causing misfortune to others becomes an act of aggression when we actively sabotage other people's plans, wants and desires.

We all understand schadenfreude, and to a greater or lesser extent we all feel that emotion. We human beings are selfish and self-centred and our view of most situations is based on what we consider to be the best for us. Earlier we looked at the relationship and balance between aggressiveness, assertiveness and passivity. Now we must also look at the balance between schadenfreude and mudita.

The opposite of schadenfreude is mudita. This is a Pali word found in Buddhist teaching, which means taking pleasure in the success and happiness of other people. An obvious example of this is when a parent is overjoyed at the success of their children. All of us want the family members whom we love to have the very highest quality of life. We also celebrate with our real friends when good things happen in their lives.

None of us would deny that these are worthy and desirable emotions to feel and display. It is worth remembering, however, that sometimes these feelings are also based on selfishness and self-centredness. When our friends are happy and successful it reflects well on us that we are moving in circles of happy and successful people. When our children succeed, we feel pleasure because it means that our family is succeeding. We probably convince ourselves that our children's success is a direct result of the genes we passed on to them and the guidance we have given them. Some parents live vicariously through their children wanting them to succeed in life, on the stage or in the professions, in a way that they may have aspired to but never achieved.

Should we completely abandon the feelings of schadenfreude and adopt only the attitude of mudita? That is probably unrealistic but, selfishly, it is certainly worth remembering that we will be in much better mental health if we celebrate the joy and happiness of others rather than being eaten up by envy and the desire for others to fail.

The next word is "kaizen." Although it is thought that this concept was developed in the United States during the 1940s, the word kaizen came from the Japanese word "kai" meaning continuous and "zen" meaning improvement. So kaizen means continuous improvement.

For most of us, when life is running smoothly we see no

reason to give it any thought. The Toyota Motor Company, however, adopted the process of kaizen. For them having a good product was never enough. Through the process of continual improvement, however small, they produce reliable, high-quality cars at the lowest possible cost. This in turn has made Toyota the largest and most successful automotive company in the world.

We, too, can use kaizen in our daily lives. Whatever job we do, we can try to do it better each time. Whatever the state of our personal finances, we can try to take better care of them. Whatever sport or hobby we participate in, we can try to do it better each time. Whatever relationships we are in, we can try to nurture them more carefully.

The final word is "shibui," a sentiment found deep in the cultural psyche of the Japanese. The word can be used in many ways but the meaning I like most is "to appreciate the imperfect beauty of things as they age." We enjoy the character of a vintage car, the warm patina of Georgian furniture and the beauty to be found in the lichen covered stonework of an old manor house.

Remembering that newness and perfection can at times be uninspiring, we should be open to appreciating the richness of human character, which in some people has been tempered in the crucible of their lives and burnished by worldly experience.

FORGIVENESS AND CATHARSIS

We all have an Achilles heel, maybe many of them as we are speaking metaphorically. My Achilles heel is forgiveness. If we do not forgive, we retain an element of control and power which may be the only aspect of the situation which we wish to cling on to. Specifically, in my case for most of my life, there was reticence to forgiving my mother for what I perceived to be her failure to have a normal maternal relationship with me. I felt that she was overly frugal with her affection and overly generous with her criticism. Some psychologists might well have attributed this feeling to my position as a "middle" child.

My belief was that she could never put my needs ahead of her own. A sure knowledge that bolstering her fragile ego was always more important than allowing me to develop my own much needed confidence. The slowly learnt understanding that she sought recognition through embellishment of the truth rather than through acting in such a way as to earn and be offered the approbation which, with her undoubted ability, she could so easily have achieved legitimately.

I blamed my mother's self-absorption for her disingenuousness and for her requirement to have total control. The situation was resolved to our mutual satisfaction when I left home just prior to my 18th birthday. From that time onwards, I was completely self-supporting not only financially but more significantly, emotionally.

Perhaps most regrettable of all is the fact that many years later, when I had children of my own, there was an opportunity to reconcile our differences and start a fresh relationship as adults.

Sadly, however, as a result of her self-defeating pride, my mother remained unchanged. Her displeasure with me was not only undiminished but was then also applied to my children. The net result was that we all lost. My children had no meaningful relationship with their only surviving grandparent. She in turn never had the close affection of one of her sons and two of her grandchildren.

For years I had heard good and worthy people talk about forgiveness. The common theme is that we forgive for our own benefit rather than for the person whom we are forgiving. It could be that when we say "forgive me" we are not so much asking for forgiveness as seeking the other person's absolution and a way of avoiding our own responsibility. Well-intentioned people have made numerous comments such as *"It is the giver who benefits from forgiveness." "It takes just as much energy to be resentful as to forgive."* Or more prosaically, *"It's not what you've eaten, it's what's eating you."*

The Oxford English dictionary defines forgiving as: "remitting a debt," "to give up any claim," "to give up resentment."

Robert Enright, a developmental psychologist at the University of Wisconsin, defines forgiveness as *"Giving up the resentment to which you are entitled and offering to the person who hurt you, friendlier attitudes to which they are not entitled."*

This now started to make sense, probably because I could see the benefit to me. It acknowledged my right to resentment. It also recognized that, although forgiveness was being offered, the recipient was not worthy of it.

Already I can hear loud cries of objection to my new-found attitude to forgiveness. Anyone coming from a purely moral or religious stance will say that there is no giving in this type of forgiveness. That I am simply maintaining the moral high ground while claiming the benefits of forgiveness.

For me, the issue of forgiveness is more about pragmatism than doing what is perceived to be morally correct. For me, forgiveness cannot and never will be an instantaneous process which allows past wrongs to disappear or be covered over by whitewash. Yet there is one way in which I can and have genuinely found the ability to forgive. It is through understanding. If I can understand what motivated someone to act in the way they did I may be able, as in the case of my mother, to give up the resentment. That is honest, genuine and worthwhile.

We all have to remember that forgiveness works in both directions. Just as others have done things to us which require our forgiveness, we have all most certainly done things to others for which we would like to receive forgiveness. Those things which we have done and said, for which we are genuinely sorry. Those things which, with the benefit of age and maturity, we wish we could change. I know that going back through my life there are many things for which I would like to apologize.

I too would like to examine my own motivation for these offences in order to explain, both to myself and to others why I did what I did on each of these occasions. No doubt, this would be a painful exercise. All of us have lied, all of us have cheated in some way and all of us have abused others.

It is not possible for me to apologize to many of the people I have abused. They are no longer accessible as a result of time, losing track and even their death. The best form of forgiveness is most certainly direct, open and honest. If we really wish to give and receive forgiveness, we need the courage to do this directly. If that is no longer possible but we still wish to go through the process of forgiveness, we can do so by visualizing the person and going through a mental conversation in which explanations are given and forgiveness transferred.

There is a Buddhist meditation in which the person meditating thinks successively about three people: one of whom they like very much, one to whom they are indifferent and a third whom they do not like. The person meditating thinks about being kind to each of these people in turn, symbolically extending a hand of genuine friendship and love. Thinking warmly and generously of the person whom we do not like sometimes takes many attempts. Repeated often enough however, feelings of hostility can be moved towards caring and affection.

We also need to extend forgiveness to ourselves. Our lives are imperfect and we have made mistakes. We have all done many things which we wish we had not done. We now carry the burden of these regrets in the form of guilt. If we can learn to forgive others, we can learn to forgive ourselves. To remember that we are human with all the imperfection that implies, and to show mercy, not only to others but also to ourselves.

There are many words which I find comforting and catharsis is one of them. It comes from the Greek meaning purification or cleansing. Through the process of catharsis we can alleviate our sadness and guilt, and in so doing can find release, atonement and emotional renewal.

INTEGRITY IN EVERYDAY LIFE

Integrity literally means being whole or complete. Our integrity relates to the wholeness of our character and how we consistently act. This includes the soundness of our dealings with other people.

We would all like other people to think of us as being a person of integrity. It is a noble concept. We would like other people to believe that we consistently speak and act with honesty and directness, that we do what is right and proper. Yet it is far more important that we should think of ourselves as being a person with integrity. This is completely possible: all we have to do is act within the framework of our own concept of integrity. Integrity engenders self-respect. If we believe we have integrity it really does not matter what other people think, but ironically, if we consistently act with integrity other people will see us as having consistency of character, which in turn is a facet of integrity.

GRATITUDE AND ATTITUDE

"Two men looked out through prison bars: one saw mud, the other saw stars" – Frederick Langbridge

An experienced commercial pilot said that when aircraft get into difficulty, the altitude of the plane is often affected by the attitude of the pilot. Whether we see the glass as being half full or half empty is not only a measure of our satisfaction in life but, more importantly, is a factor which we can consciously control for our own benefit. We can choose whether to be pessimistic and disillusioned or upbeat and optimistic. This choice is important because it directly affects the quality of our lives. It affects our level of happiness and our physical well-being.

A cranio-sacral therapist in London starts all his healing sessions by affirming that the patient's condition will improve. He ensures that they fully believe and expect to make improvement. He advises them to anticipate and look forward to recovery. He says that this always works favourably, but that the opposite can also be true. That is, if a patient is constantly reminding themselves of their pain and expects their condition to deteriorate, it will probably do so.

Recently a young woman in a wheelchair attended a public meeting. Her legs appeared to have no movement or strength in them. It was difficult for her to manoeuvre her chair around in the small, relatively crowded room. When other people were standing and walking around, she had to strain her neck backwards in order to look up.

This woman could well have indulged in self-pity. She could have become bitter and withdrawn, feeling that she had been robbed of all the joys of a fully mobile young womanhood. No doubt she has many regrets about her condition but the person we all saw was truly amazing.

She exuded a positive attitude and certainly had all the confidence you would expect from a beautiful young woman. It appeared that she had accepted her physical condition as being different from the majority but she was absolutely determined to participate in everything which appealed to her. She smiled readily and her face was full of enthusiasm. She spoke with pride about the fact that she runs her own business. She had obviously decided to concentrate on all the good things she had going for her.

As we progress through each day, we encounter minor difficulties, things which block our path or cause minor irritation. Life also presents us with very substantial problems and difficult situations. There is the true story of a man who had been under a great deal of stress at work. The more his boss applied pressure to him, the more inadequate he felt, and that this in turn exacerbated the problem. He said that while standing at a tube station the thought passed through his mind that there was a simple way to end his suffering.

He then thought about his loving, supportive wife and about his children, whom he loved dearly. He knew that they loved, wanted and needed him. Of course, his job was important but his life and his place in the family was far more important. Unfortunately, we all tend to respond to immediate pressures and sometimes lose sight of the larger picture.

While this man had not been serious about committing suicide, the fact that this thought had even passed through his mind proved to be really valuable to him. He decided to mentally step back and look at his whole situation. He wrote out a list of all the wonderful things he had in his life, starting with his family. He remembered his long-term friends and even the enjoyment he felt every time he took his playful dog for a walk in the woods. He thought about the enormous pleasure he received from his hobby of walking in the Lake District. Armed with the understanding that his life contained so much that was worthwhile and beautiful, he set about analysing his problems and working out a strategy to deal with them.

Rather than waiting for a crisis to occur, it is a good exercise for all of us to regularly think about all of the good things in our lives. To be grateful for the abundance we have in our lives, things which we may well take for granted but which are so valuable to us.

Today, I am grateful for the fact that I could swing my legs out of bed and walk to the window where I could see fresh dew on a little patch of grass and hear the birds singing. I am grateful for the fact that I have a bathroom with hot running water and a flushing lavatory. I am amazed and grateful for the wonder of electricity which lights my world and boils my kettle.

I am grateful for the people in my life, including my immediate family and those people whom I love and care about, such as my friends and social contacts. I know that without them my life would be completely empty. I value the fact that I also contribute to the lives of these people.

I am constantly amazed by and grateful for the endless beauty of nature. My interests and musical tastes have evolved and changed throughout my life but I am grateful for the traditional jazz which enlivened my youth. In later life, my gratitude goes to Brahms, Handel and Mozart who had the inspiration and genius to write the sublime choral music which can now transport me to a state of pure rapture.

I am fully aware of, and grateful for, the fact that my life is a privileged one. There is an abundance of food from which I can choose. I am lucky to receive first-rate dental and medical attention and I fully appreciate the warmth of my house and my comfortable bed.

As the song most beautifully sung by Aled Jones, says:

Count your blessings one by one,
When dawn appears and day has just begun;
They will light your heart with happiness
Make each hour bright and bring you gladness
Count your blessings one by one
When twilight falls and toil of day is done
And in sweet dreams they'll come again to you
If you will count your blessings each day through.

Count your blessings while you may,
For we are here but little time to stay;
All around are hearts sincere and true
Lovely things abound just waiting for you
Count your blessings while you may
The big or small, whichever comes your way
For then you'll find this world a place of love
If you will count your blessings from above.[3]

In the United States, there is a foundation devoted to undertaking "Random Acts of Kindness". As individuals we may or may not agree with the formalising of such an organisation but the concept is beautiful and completely sound. As we go through our daily lives, we are presented with so many opportunities to make someone else's life just that little bit better.

We can look someone in the eye, we can smile and we can acknowledge our fellow human beings. We can if we wish also do more than this. We can help complete strangers in some small way, such as helping carry a suitcase up the stairs in the underground. We can take the opportunity to support others rather than merely hurrying through life with our blinkers on.

This is not a matter of becoming a roving "good Samaritan" whose working life is given over to doing worthwhile deeds. It is

3. This poem is sung by Aled Jones in his CD *"Higher"* from R Morgan/ E Temple

a way of accepting the opportunity to undertake small acts of kindness to others when the opportunity arises. Although this should not be our motive for offering kindness, it does have a symbiotic effect which enriches our own lives.

In parallel with this, I would advocate that we should undertake "Random acts of Gratitude." When anything pleases us or when someone has been courteous, supportive or kind to us, we should not only acknowledge our gratitude to them but we should feel the gratitude within ourselves. Throughout our day we should constantly be aware of how fortunate we are. We should acknowledge and be grateful for the abundant goodness which comes to us.

PROBLEM SOLVING - DECISION MAKING

Every day of our lives we have to make small choices. What clothes are we going to wear on that day, and will we take the bus or walk to work? Small decisions are easy to make because the consequences are not particularly significant. The greater the effect of the outcome of a decision, the harder it is to decide what to do. If we are faced with the prospect of leaving a secure job and starting our own business, or whether or not to make a major investment such as buying a house, we need to think very carefully about the pros and cons.

The importance and long-term impact of the decisions we make do, of course, vary, but the principle is exactly the same. We have to ask ourselves, what are the advantages of doing something and what are the disadvantages? What are the potential gains and what are the potential losses? The following example is one which could apply to many people but, more importantly, the process by which the decision is reached can be applied to almost any situation.

Let us take the example of someone who is thinking about moving from one job to another. The first question to ask would be, why am I are even considering a move? What is the potential advantage in making a move? The answer could be any one or a combination of the following. The new job would pay more, would be more interesting, would have greater prospects or would be in another city where I would like to live.

What would be the disadvantages of taking the new job? There is always the risk that the new work environment will not be as enjoyable or as comfortable as the present one. The company to which you are thinking of moving is known to be a high-pressure organisation and there are even concerns about its long-term financial viability.

Then it is necessary to look more closely at the situation you are currently in. What are the pros and cons of this job? It could be that you really like or really dislike the people you are working with. Is this situation likely to be long term? In other words the people you either like or dislike could well move on in the near future anyway. Financially, your existing company has been quite fair to you over the past couple of years. It is a well established company and there is every indication that it will operate for many years to come. If you're looking for something more exciting or a new challenge, are there any opportunities in your existing company which would give you that?

Faced with any type of decision, we have to avoid the feeling that something is in some way pre-ordained and that we have no control over it. We have to avoid taking the simple option of just yielding to whatever pressure we are under. Instead, we have to look at such situations for what they are. A situation or problem to which we have to find a solution. Adding confusion to the problem itself is the fact that when many people try to make decisions they do not really focus on the elements of decision-making.

To really think about an issue, it is best to find a place and time at which you will have no other distractions. Then write out columns of advantages and disadvantages for each of the options. This is a simple way of clarifying some of the issues. Without doing this, it is too easy to be distracted by the emotional components without giving full consideration to the hard facts.

If it is a decision between two options, you should end up with four written columns. A column of pros and a column of cons, for each of the two options. Sometimes there may be additional options, in which case it is necessary to look at the pros and cons for each of these as well. Then it is worth putting these in order of significance or value. For example, if you really want to move to a new city, then you give this such a substantial value that it overrides many of the other issues.

Most decisions are easier to make with more information and less uncertainty. We must find out as much as possible about the various options available to us. One way of doing this is to confide in our friends and ask for their opinions and advice. When we do this, we have to be sure that the advice they are giving us is based on what is best for us rather than what might be to their advantage or what they think we wish to hear. We also have to use our own judgment as to how much common sense there is in their advice. If, using the example above, we are asking several people who work for the new company what they think of it, we may get differing answers depending on their own circumstances. We should, nevertheless, be able to pick up an overall feeling about that company and whether or not it would suit us.

This formula of decision-making can be applied to almost every decision we make in life, including the formation, or dissolution, of relationships. A key factor in making decisions is to really understand ourselves. Not to be drawn in by what is temporarily exciting and superficial but to know what the real objective is and what is right for us.

In most decisions there is an element of uncertainty, which in turn means that there is an element of risk. The more important a decision is, the greater the risk. The greater the risk, the greater the fear involved, not only in making a wrong decision but in making any decision at all. So just as we make decisions every day, we take risks every day. Most of these risks are fairly insignificant. For example, if we risk not taking an umbrella on a cloudy day, the worst that can happen is that we will get wet. Other decisions involve a greater degree of risk. Playing any sport has some potential for injury, with the level of risk increasing according to the severity of the potential injury. Rock climbing and skydiving carry a higher level of risk than football.

The fact remains that, in order to do anything or achieve anything, we must overcome fear and take some risks. If we want to form new relationships, build a business or paddle down the Amazon, it will involve fear and risk. The logical thing is to analyse the potential risks and then to do everything possible to minimise them. To minimise the potential for harm while maximising the potential benefit.

Sometimes our desire for something is so great that, through courage, we can overcome huge obstacles. Sometimes we have a "gut feeling" that seems to override common sense and logic. Most of the great achievers have overcome apparently insurmountable obstacles. Through strength of personality and sheer determination they have battled their way to success. I applaud these people and am the first to recognise that without them the world would be a very static place. I am also aware of the fact that for every Charles Lindbergh there is an Amelia Earhart. For every Stanley, there is a Shackleton.

The counterbalance to the purely logical thinker is the person with cognitive flexibility, the person with intuition. It may well be that intuition is simply a subconscious process of analysis. If after careful analysis, decisions still hang in the balance, it may simply be worth letting our intuition takeover. If it genuinely feels right for us to do something, that is another choice which we can follow.

JUDGMENT AND COMMON SENSE

It has been said that common sense is not very common. If it was, everyone would have it. But common sense is a simple term for everyday judgment, one of the most valuable human skills we can develop in life. It has nothing to do with academic intelligence and a great deal to do with our day-to-day lives. It is the sum of how well, apparently intuitively, we understand all of the situations in which we find ourselves and how capably we deal with them.

Good drivers are taught to look well ahead, inexperienced drivers tend to look little further ahead than the car in front of them. If we take in the larger picture of what is around us and the consequences of even the most minor action, we will be better prepared to avoid problems and enjoy advantageous situations. This is not to suggest that we should go through life playing it like a game of chess and planning every move. The analogy is, however, useful in that being aware of the potential outcome of different choices can help us get things right more often.

Common sense and good judgment are relevant every time we make a decision. Some people avoid making decisions because that in turn ensures that they will never make a mistake. Avoiding taking a decision is a mistake itself. Everyone makes mistakes throughout their lives. When we do make a mistake, we must set about rectifying it as quickly as possible. Then, so long as we are aware of why we made that mistake, we can learn from it and ensure that we do not make a similar mistake again.

Part of common sense and good judgment is developing an awareness of other people. Being tuned in to how they will feel and react to various situations including what we say and what we do. Just as we react to other people's behaviour, so they react to ours. This does not mean that we have to compromise our principles in any way. It simply means that we must be aware of how our words and actions affect other people. We always know why we say and do things but must constantly maintain an awareness of how other people are interpreting what we say and do.

For many years I worked in London but my head office was in North America. Due to the time difference and for the sake of economy most of our dealings were by e-mail. Sometimes I received very abrupt answers to questions or suggestions. My interpretation of this was that head office was being rude and dismissive. I later learned that they too felt that some of my correspondence was somewhat offhand.

Whenever we talked on the phone the situation was better. We enjoyed the personal contact, and being able to speak to someone, as opposed to exchanging e-mails, allows us to hear the intonation of their voice. It allows us to pick up subtle cues such as pauses and hesitations. It allows us to hear excitement and enthusiasm, all of which are lost in the abbreviated practicality of an e-mail or text. Even face-to-face we have to be sure that what we say and do is perceived and interpreted correctly in the spirit in which it is meant.

Avoiding misunderstandings will allow us to avoid a huge number of petty problems. Put more positively, when we understand other people and what is motivating them, it is much easier to deal with them. We need to realise that other people have pressures in their lives, and often their way of dealing with us simply reflects the stresses impinging on their lives at that time.

Although our common sense is apparently intuitive, it has been learnt consciously or subconsciously and like any other skill can be further developed and improved. If there are any parts of our daily lives which are not working smoothly, we can think about them and plan ways in which to make improvements. We can learn to act and react effectively.

CHARACTER JUDGMENT

Over the years, I have made the mistake of considering myself to be a pretty good judge of character. One look at a person or a situation and I thought that my lightning quick brain could sum them up instantly. Let me give you some examples of how mistaken I was.

Flicking through the channels on television I saw a rather unusual woman. She had a completely unpronounceable name and was wearing strange ethnic clothes. I knew immediately that this interview would be of no interest to me and switched to another channel.

About two weeks later a friend sent me a clipping from the London Evening Standard. She said, "You will be really interested to read this article about a truly remarkable woman. Her name is Camila Batmanghelidjh. She is the founder of an amazing organisation called Kids Company. She gives support to some of the most underprivileged and potentially violent children in London. Her philosophy is completely new. She says the problem is that we have hugely underestimated the horrific abuse and violence that many of these children have suffered, growing up in deprived neighbourhoods. What these children need most is someone who genuinely cares about them and can in turn offer realistic guidance.

It was true I was interested in this view of children, whom in the past I might have regarded as being intrinsically bad, and for whom I could now have some understanding, sympathy and appreciation.

In another situation, I was acquainted for more than 20 years with a rather cantankerous old woman. She was already about 70 when I first met her. She was the honorary secretary of a political dinner club which had a number of very high profile members. My assumption had always been that she was a rather self-opinionated hanger-on who enjoyed contact with these influential people.

That was until I read her obituary in the newspaper. The first thing I noticed was the photograph of her taken at the age of 19. She had been a beautiful young woman who married a handsome naval officer. She had led a truly energetic and worthwhile life, and it turned out that it was she who had started the club which became a thriving centre for political debate. She was certainly not a hanger-on. The Daily Telegraph described her as "An intellectual powerhouse embroiled in the literary, political and social life of Britain for more than 60 years"

This was a salutary lesson for me and a reminder that many of us, motivated by our insecurities, ascribe our own failings to other people.

On another occasion, I attended a luncheon meeting in a smart club on St. James. I had a business guest with me and was rather puffed up for the occasion. To my horror, we were seated at a table with four other people, one of whom struck me as being a bit shabby. He was an elderly man, rather quiet and uninteresting. It shames me to say that when I ordered wine for the meal I felt annoyed to be sharing it with people whom I did not know.

Sometime after this lunch I read this man's obituary in The Daily Telegraph. His name was John Patton and his story was truly remarkable.

At the outbreak of war, he was living in Canada. He applied to join the Canadian Army but was rejected on medical grounds. He could, with a clear conscience, have returned to a comfortable life training to be a lawyer in Halifax, Nova Scotia. Instead, he boarded a ship and came to England.

In the UK, he applied to join the British Army. He was accepted, although it was clearly understood that he was not physically able to engage in active service. The British Army did, however, suggest that they had a "little job" which he might be able to do for them. Bomb disposal.

For the next four years, John Patton faced the possibility and even the probability of being blown up. Every time he went out to work there was the chance that he would be killed or maimed. Many of his work colleagues suffered this fate.

On one occasion, he was called to defuse a large and particularly unstable bomb in the grounds of a hospital in Guildford. Despite the urgency to defuse this bomb, the chances of doing so successfully were considered to be minimal. It was potentially a suicide mission. With immense courage and skill, he did miraculously defuse the bomb.

As a result of this action he was awarded the George Cross, Britain's highest award for non-combat gallantry. This man had more courage in his little finger than I have in my entire being. This man, whom I thought shabby and with whom I had not wanted to share my wine.

I would like to be able to tell you that I am a reformed character, that I no longer make quick judgments about people. To be honest, I cannot truly say this, but I have learnt to take a second look at people remembering that the old were once young, attractive, energetic and relevant.

Sometimes people do not make it easy for us to get to know them. Their own shyness, insecurities and suspicions create defences which we simply do not make the effort to overcome. When I meet people like this, I remember our wonderful labrador. On walks down country lanes we would often find blackberries growing wild – always protected by the sharpest of thorns. She was able to suck off fruit, carefully avoiding all the prickles. How she did this I do not know, but, just as she had the skill to get at the good parts without being hurt, so can we.

I am convinced that everyone has something interesting about them, but we do sometimes have to make an effort to bypass the thorns in order to reveal it. Winston Churchill thought the same thing when he wrote: *"Inside the heart of everyman there is treasure. We only have to find it."*

And John Masefield said it most beautifully when he wrote:

> *"I have seen flowers come in stony places,*
> *And kind things done by men with ugly faces,*
> *And the gold cup won by the worst horse at the races,*
> *So I trust, too."*

LISTENING IS AS IMPORTANT AS SPEAKING

"*You cannot truly listen to anyone and do anything else at the same time*," said Dr. M. Scott Peck, author of "The Road Less Travelled."

When we speak, we want other people to listen to us. We want them to really hear what we are saying and to understand what we are trying to convey to them. We want to feel that we have their full attention and that they are interested in what we are saying. What we do not want is to feel that people are only listening superficially, that their mind is partly on other things.

We can give people the gift of listening to them. Sometimes this is a real gift as in the case of an old pensioner who engages conversation at the checkout of a supermarket. We all have a need to be heard and the more isolated we feel, the more valuable this becomes.

Whenever we approach someone in a service industry, what we really want is to be heard. The outcome of a conversation may be the same but we do want to feel that our concern was understood and taken seriously. We want bank staff, car repair depots and hardware stores to understand our needs as a customer.

So far I have only talked about listening in respect to fairly mundane things such as getting the car repaired. As soon as we become emotionally involved, it is far more important to all of us that our listener should be fully engaged.

Like many clichés, there is much truth in the fact that some women confide in their hairdresser. One hairdresser has the theory that being touched immediately creates a sense of intimacy. He goes on to say that, although he is physically touching his client, she in turn is looking at him in the mirror. To her, the hairdresser appears to be several feet away, at a sufficiently safe distance not to be a threat. So there is a paradoxical juxtaposition of both intimacy and distance. He goes on to say that he believes many women come to him, or visit therapists, not so much for the specific treatment being offered as for the chance to talk. In turn, he rewards their openness with confidentiality and is in no way condemnatory or judgmental.

Every single one of us is guilty on occasions of failing to listen fully to other people. My wife used to jokingly accuse me of having selective hearing and it is true that there were times when I "switched off." How much better it would have been if I had learned to listen, not necessarily with the concentration and intensity of a musician, but with genuine care as to what was being said.

As listeners, it is important that we do not in any way interrupt the flow of what someone is trying to say. Even being overly empathetic can dilute what is being said or alter the course of what they need to say. We should allow people to express fully everything that they need to say. We should always resist the temptation to "fix" the problem by quickly jumping in with our own ideas and solutions. We should avoid "piggy-backing" on someone else's story. By this I mean that if someone tells us about an event which is important to them, we should not deflect attention away from them by immediately coming up with a parallel or stronger example of something that happened to us.

If tears come, we should allow them to flow without unnecessary intervention. Tears of emotion have a different chemical make-up to those generated purely for the lubrication of the eye. Crying is more cathartic than stifling our emotions. Crying gives expression and produces release, which we as listeners should allow to take place.

There are groups which practice "co-counselling." This involves one person speaking, usually in response to a given question, without any verbal or physical interruption from the listener. When the speaker stops speaking, the listener will recount, as accurately as possible, what they heard the speaker say. The two people will then change roles, with the first speaker now listening to the other person.

It is quite an interesting exercise to practise "active listening" when there are no emotions involved. If a friend of yours has just returned from holiday and has been telling you all about it, you can do more than merely nod occasionally. You could for example say "Yes that really sounds like fun, driving down the narrow winding roads of the Amalfi coast. You sound as if you really enjoyed walking through all those steep, narrow passageways in the old mediaeval towns. Did you enjoy lots of the Mediterranean salads about which we hear so much?"

We can use elements of co-counselling in our everyday lives. When someone is speaking to us, we can give them the freedom to continue without interrupting or hijacking their story. If someone is emotional, we can listen to them and hear their pain. We may wish to show empathy or to rush in and find solutions but is more important to let the speaker release all of the things they have to say. We can acknowledge that we are actively listening through non-evaluative responses such as "Hmm," "really," and "I see," Sometimes we can use the same techniques as a psychotherapist. That is to ask a questions "which open the door" and invite a response. Questions such as. "How do you feel about that?", "Would you like to talk about it? and "Tell me more about that."

Anyone who manages people should be aware that just listening goes a long way towards solving problems. People want to be heard.

In Austria in 1880, Dr Joseph Breuer, a contemporary of Sigmund Freud, was experimenting with a new form of treatment which in time would form the basis of psychoanalysis. In a well documented case of a patient, known as "Anna O," she referred to this treatment as, *The Talking Cure.*

Sharing problems goes some way to easing them. To give someone the gift of release and unburdening, we must allow them to speak freely and to be truly heard. We have two ears and one mouth and it has been suggested that we should use them in the same ratio.

LIFELONG LEARNING

"Teachers open the door, but you must enter by yourself" –
Chinese proverb.

From Roman times through feudalism and into the early 19th
century the dominant way of life was agrarian. The schools and
universities which did exist at these times taught few subjects
other than reading, writing and Latin. The clergy were the most
highly educated group, but even their learning tended to be
restricted to theological matters. It was the tremendous upheaval
of the Industrial Revolution and the emergence of a growing
demand for technology that necessitated and promoted broader
education for the laity.

Men like Dr Arnold of "Tom Brown's Schooldays" added
interest and diversity to the school curriculum. Sadly much of
that wisdom was lost in the post-war urgency to pass exams at all
cost, leaving teachers insufficient time to show the richness of
their subject.

As someone who did not enjoy school and did not find
schoolwork easy, I am quite surprised by the transition which has
taken place in my life. A complete shift away from thinking that
learning was boring and difficult to finding that new knowledge,
which interests me, is one of the most important and pleasurable
aspects of my life.

The key is probably to be found in the phrase "knowledge
which interests me." School for me was a place where I was forced
to work on subjects which did not interest me and which
appeared to have little relevance to my life. The fact that I was not
good at learning in the way that the school required, meant that

for me, school and learning (which were synonymous) were painful and to be avoided. An expression I often heard as a child was that "schooldays are the happiest days of your lives." I can honestly say that frightened me. If this was the best that life had to offer, there was very little to commend it for me.

Looking back, I know that from the age of 20 onwards my life has been increasingly happy. Just like school, there have been many times when I had to work on projects which were difficult and did not interest me. The difference is that my life contained wonderful counterbalances which did interest and excite me. Some of that interest has come to me in the form of new knowledge about a whole host of subjects ranging from history and architecture to sociology and music.

Not necessarily a formal knowledge of these subjects. For example, I love visiting National Trust properties and am awestruck by the wonder of old churches and cathedrals. Over the years I have gradually learnt a little bit about different styles and can appreciate some architectural detail. That is quite different to being an architect. When I left school, and even now, I did not have the educational background or willpower to study the very difficult course required to qualify as an architect. Put another way, we do not have to be a trained musician to enjoy music, just as we do not have to be an athlete to enjoy watching sports. But the more we learn about any of these things, the more we are able to appreciate and enjoy them.

Many years ago I was attending a six-week intensive language course in the South of France. For me, and for most of the other students, this was a work-related requirement which we found to be difficult and demanding. The most enthusiastic student was a retired American lawyer. He was financially secure and had no reason to learn French other than his desire to do so. Even more astonishing was the fact that he was suffering from terminal cancer. For him, learning French was a pleasure in itself. For him, there was no particular goal or destination, only the wish to absorb yet more information which interested him.

Reading almost anything, in any genre, gives us new insights. Facts and science increase our understanding, while biography and fiction allow us to catch a glimpse of other peoples' lives. To see that we are not alone in our fears and trepidation or in our sadness and joy. Through reading, we may also experience emotions at a greater intensity than our own lives will ever present to us.

The journalist Rachel Pugh interviewed the polymath, Sir Jonathan Miller, who trained as a medical doctor but went on to have a highly creative theatrical career, which included directing many operas. She quotes Miller as saying. *"At the age of 15, I encountered a rather miraculous teacher (at St Paul's school) called Sid Pask. I'm sure that Mr Pask's influence is partly responsible for the fact that I make no distinction between entertainment and illumination."* How enviable to have the wonderful brain of a man like Jonathan Miller. Even more enviable, however, is to have teachers like Mr Pask. Or someone like Adam Hart-Davis, who taught at Eton College, whose obvious enjoyment and enthusiasm for his subject is so great that we willingly immerse ourselves in his stream of knowledge.

Sometimes, foundations are laid on which we come to build many years later. Having been a choirboy and server throughout my childhood, I must have attended hundreds of Anglican services. This was fortunately at a time when the King James version of both the Bible and prayer book were still being used. Quite apart from the message they delivered, the beauty of the language in which they are written permeated my mind. I am in no doubt that this has contributed substantially to my love of the English language.

In a school environment, we take what is given to us in the way of teaching and guidance. As adults we have the choice of seeking out not only the subjects that are of interest to us, but also the people who can enthuse us. I personally owe a great debt of gratitude to the late Kenneth Clark who wrote and presented an amazing television series called "Civilisation." Through this series, I learnt to find pleasure in art, architecture and history. The pleasure was gained because those of us who watched the series were presented with information that was easy to understand and interesting.

The rarefied and somewhat stultifying world of the arts with all its pretensions had been opened for me and explained in such a way that it truly changed my life. From that time on, not only did I find additional interest in the arts but I learnt that by opening my eyes and being receptive to new things, there was so much more in life in which to find pleasure.

This may sound high-brow but it is not. The object of our interest may or may not appeal to the majority of other people. Opera is obviously less popular in numerical terms than pop music. That does not make one more or less valuable than the other. Choosing eclectically gives us the greatest range of interests and pleasure.

The primary concern of television producers is to entertain. In turn they produce the kind of entertainment which is most in demand and will therefore yield the greatest revenue from advertisers. The good news is that there is now a huge choice of very worth while programmes covering nature, history, the arts and science. It is our choice whether to spend our television watching hours on quality material or waste it on dross.

Similarly, the Internet now gives us access to almost unlimited information. Vast amounts of knowledge are available in our homes within seconds, but again it is up to us to use this wonderful medium sensibly and to seek out nuggets of wisdom.

The important thing is the willingness to take at least a few steps down many avenues in turn. It is that which keeps us interested in life and may even lead us to something of wonder and beauty.

"*Time ripens all things, no man is born wise*" – Miguel de Cervantes

SELF-ACTUALIZATION

Throughout our lives, but especially towards the end of them, we wish to feel a sense of accomplishment. We wish to feel that we have become all that we were capable of becoming, and that we have achieved and realised all or much of our potential. That in turn requires the maturity to acknowledge that many of life's circumstances were outside our control. The maturity to recognize and understand, with the benefit of hindsight, the wrong decisions we made and why we made them.

Achieving a state of self-actualisation means we have reached an appropriate state of contentment and self-satisfaction. An authenticity which leads to an acceptance and enjoyment of the person we are. A willingness, rather than a denial, to embrace the full truth of our lives recognizing our achievements and contributions within the framework of our circumstances. A disinhibited frame of mind which gives us an ability to acknowledge and to reveal our full and true identity.

It is estimated that only about 2% of the population are ever in a state of self-actualization. This is very sad because many people do have the right to feel more self-satisfied – but it may be that they are overly self-critical. Perhaps they fall into the trap of comparison in which, using inappropriate criteria, they see themselves as less successful than other people.

Paradoxically and commendably, many of the emotionally healthy people who do reach the state of self-actualization do not remain static in this apparent sate of Nirvana. They sincerely wish to give something back to society. They take pleasure in seeing other people develop and prosper, and willingly give their support in any way that they can to make this happen.

When someone is fully self-actualized they have moved beyond petty jealousy and paranoia. Far from feeling threatened or diminished by the success of others, they take a healthy pleasure in seeing other people's growth and happiness. In this state of transcendence, there is a genuine desire to see other people raised up as high as possible, so they too may achieve self-actualization.

LEVEL 8 – TRANCENDENCE

Helping others so self-actualize

LEVEL 8 - TRANCENDENCE

Many of the rich turn their energy and abilities to charitable causes. The ultimate goal and ultimate reward of great wealth (or great ability) can be the opportunity to be truly altruistic, to improve the quality of life for many other people. To support education, medical science, beneficial projects in the developing world and to be supportive of the arts. Good examples of these are the foundations established by Andrew Carnegie, the Melon family and now Warren Buffet together with Bill Gates.

On a different but equally important level, many people give substantially of themselves. They work tirelessly for charities and a host of organisations dedicated to supporting their communities and the less fortunate. There are numerous unsung heroes especially in the caring professions such as ambulance crews, care workers and hospital staff. Many teachers go well beyond the basic requirements of their job and strive to give their charges the best possible start in life.

I count myself fortunate when I look back through my life and know that there were people who undoubtedly supported and mentored me. Their guidance and example was, without question, a generous and much valued gift.

Transcendence quite literally means "going beyond." Those who leave a worthwhile legacy to their families, to random individuals and to society in general are the true achievers. Those who give more to the world than they take from it reach the pinnacle of life and the very top of Maslow's pyramid.

FINAL THOUGHTS

Some choices for us to consider.

After the horrors of the Second World War, a veteran wrote, *"Peace has brought many pleasures, but nothing as powerful as that passion for survival in wartime."*[4]

What we all need is some of that passion. A sense that we want to win the ultimate prize of a full and worthwhile life. An understanding that in order for us to achieve this we must give as fully as we receive. An understanding that global issues are our own personal issues.

Our lives should not merely be a journey towards the final destination of death. The more freedom we have or can obtain in life, the greater is our control. We can squander the choices that freedom affords us or we can set out to live the most rewarding life we can. Life can and should be pleasurable. The happier we are, the more we will spread a sense of happiness around us. We have the gift to bring happiness to other people. Human nature is such that whatever small seeds of happiness we sow, are usually rewarded with an abundant harvest.

We all want to be fortunate in our lives. Luck does play a part but also implies that we are undeserving of both the benefits and the disadvantages resulting purely from luck. How fortunate or unfortunate we are is frequently dependent on the choices we have made, the judgment we have employed and the energy we have expended.

We can choose to live with an attitude of acceptance and love,

4. *The Forgotten Soldier,* Guy Sajer Fitzhenry, Whiteside

or to perpetuate ethnic, national and personal enmity.

We can choose to be financially responsible for ourselves or we can optimistically assume that we will somehow be taken care of.

We can choose to be in a loving relationship or we can unrealistically pursue the wrong targets and fail to find companionship.

We can choose whether or not to believe in a divine being and how to live in harmony with our beliefs.

We can choose to keep our bodies as healthy as possible or to ignore and abuse them.

We can decide what morality and ethics mean to us and practise what we believe to be right or consciously decide to do otherwise.

We can choose to have the strength of confidence or to feel imposed on by the world in general.

We can choose to be excited about all the wonderful new things we can learn about or sit contentedly on our plateau of understanding.

We can choose whether or not to be aware of our own mental health and to actively maintain it in the same way that we can keep physically well.

We can choose to seek out beauty and to rejoice in everything we find wonderful or we can restrict our view to ugliness and sadness.

We can choose to seek out and mix with people whom we find joyful and uplifting or we can allow ourselves to be exhausted by other peoples' negativity.

We can choose to be prepared for death – the death of people whom we love and our own death – or we can try to ignore it.

We can choose to exercise our right to the freedom of our own thinking and decide on our own actions or we can be a prisoner of outward influences.

We can choose to be active stewards of our world or we can consciously leave a legacy of environmental issues to the next generation.

We can choose to be happy, or not! Happiness should be our "default" setting.

Everything which has been written in this book is about recognising that we have choices and that it is up to us to exercise our choice. Having choice means that we have freedom. It is the goal to which most of us aspire through the intermediary of wealth.

In North Africa, there are the Berber people who call themselves Imazighen. Translated this means "the free people." They are nomadic goat herders who in material terms are desperately poor, but as they value freedom above everything else, they feel they already have what the rest of the world is trying to achieve.

No one and nothing can make you happy except you yourself. We do not necessarily need to know much in life but we do need to know how to make ourselves happy.

ABOUT THE AUTHOR

Paul W. King, a graduate of the University of Alberta, was born in India to British parents, and has lived, worked and travelled extensively in many parts of the world. He lived for more than twenty years in Canada and the USA.

For several years he was involved in taking oil and gas related trade missions to many South-east Asian and Pacific Rim countries. He has worked for large corporations, including the professional photography department of Kodak Canada Ltd, Canadian government trade organizations, and spent over 20 years in various business related consular positions in Europe.

The author has spent a lifetime meeting, and subconsciously studying, many new people in a variety of cultures. He attributes his undoubted interest in, and understanding of, human nature to his own search for answers and the knowledge passed on to him by so many wise and interesting people in so many different environments.

As an experienced speaker, and former professional photographer, Paul now writes travel articles and coaches others in giving talks and presentations.